- Get Sarah's FREE we
- How To Plan Your Fi
  www.sarahcordiner
- Join the Facebook gr... .... to Edupreneur'
- See the back page of this book for your FREE ECOURSE

Author: Sarah Cordiner

Title: The Theory & Principles of Creating Effective Training Courses

Subtitle: What To Do Before Creating Your Course

Subjects: Education; Adult Education; Learning Theory and Practice; Curriculum Design and Development

Disclaimer: The material in this publication is of the nature of general comment only, and does not represent professional advice. It is not intended to provide specific guidance for particular circumstances, and it should not be relied upon as the basis for any decision to take action or not take action on any matter which it covers. Readers should obtain professional advice where appropriate, before making any such decision. To the maximum extent permitted by law, the author and publisher disclaim all responsibility and liability to any person, arising directly or indirectly from any person taking action or not taking action based on the information in this publication.

The moral rights of the author have been asserted.

The Theory and Principles of Creating Effective Training Courses

The Edupreneur's Guide

The Theory & Principles of **Creating Effective Training Courses**

What To Do Before Creating Your Course

SARAH CORDINER

The Theory and Principles of Creating Effective Training Courses

ACKNOWLEDGEMENTS

"This one is for my history teacher, who as a result of being the world's biggest jerk, set me on a journey to learn how NOT to be an appalling teacher.

It's also for my art teacher, who gave me the gift of efficacy that has resulted in a life dedicated to positively transformational education.

And finally, it's for the manager (Jackie Baitup) who believed in me enough to give me my first ever training job many years ago. Without her faith and encouragement, my education business may not have been born.

It's also for my husband who is my rock. Without his never ending support, I wouldn't be able to do what I do."

The Theory and Principles of Creating Effective Training Courses

TABLE OF CONTENTS

ACKNOWLEDGEMENTS...v
TABLE OF CONTENTS vii
Introduction 1
The Learning Revolution is Here..9
Avoid the Dark Side of the Course Creation Industry 14
Reality Check: Are you Ready for Teaching Online?............ 31
Efficacious Education 37
The Efficacy Effect Model 51
Building Educational Efficacy 59
Informing Your Practise with the Theory of Adult Learning
.... 73
The Principle of Self-Direction..................................... 75
Embrace Individuality 83
The Mistake of Over-Independence............................ 86
The Principle of Motivation in Learning 89
Strategies for Motivating and Engaging the Disengaged. 98
Re-engage Efficacy of Disengaged Learners........................109
The Principle of Learning by Doing 113
The Learning Principle of Context.............................. 118
The Learning Principle Of Relevance And Readiness 125
The Learning Principle of Contextualisation 129
The Learning Principle of Experience........................137

The Learning Principle of Reflection	143
The Learning Principle of the Senses	155
Get In the 'Mode'	157
Know Your Global vs. Your Analytical	165
Capture Hearts and Minds	169
Nourish Both Sides of the Brain	173
The Learning Principle of Practise	181
The Learning Principle of Personal Development	187
Plan for Lifelong Learning	191
Lifelong Learning in the Workplace	207
The Learning Principle of Behaviourism	213
The Learning Principle of Constructivism	223
PART TWO	225
PRE-PLANNING FOR YOUR COURSE CREATION	225
Introduction	226
The Learning Principle of Involvement	227
Define Your Target Group	233
Accredited Or Non-Accredited?	239
Identify the Purpose of Your Learning Program	241
The Different Dimensions of Competence	245
Plan Your Course Specifications	251
Prepare For Stakeholders	257
Plan for Stakeholder Needs	261

The Learning Principle of Learner-Centred Education	263
Identify Target Learner Group Needs	267
Identify Individual Learner Needs	269
Plan for Course Creation in Corporate and Workplace Training	273
Determine the Learning Timeframes	279
Conclusion	285
Connect With Sarah	289
About The Author	290
REFERENCES	298
The Blurb	302
FREE ECOURSE:	305
GET A SECOND COURSE FOR FREE	305

INTRODUCTION

"A universal human need is to improve and progress in life. Nobody wants to think their life will be worse tomorrow than it is today. Within that concept is our hunger to learn."
Shovlin

Like most adolescents, I had no idea what I wanted to do when I left school. But I did have an insatiable appetite for learning and working.

My father was a hard-working, self-employed builder, and there was nothing I loved more than helping him out with everything, from his paperwork, PA duties, mixing the perfect concrete, wall-papering old ladies' houses to out-right demolition jobs. (I liked those ones a bit too much!) He would teach me, and I would hungrily learn.

I wanted to know how everything worked, yet I hated school. How could a young person, so naturally hungry for learning, be so opposed to formal schooling?

Then one day in 1994, this question was answered for me in a way that cemented the direction my life would take forever....

Once upon a time...

That day it was unusually warm for England. The sun poured through the classroom window, spewing over my exercise book as I scribbled down the date with my HB staedtler pencil. I was swinging backwards in my chair at the back of Mr. Burkett's history class. We were learning about King Henry the Eighth and his wives.

The mousy-haired girl next to me was proudly reciting some poem that she said helped her remember who all of Henry's wives were and how they had died. I looked around the room with increasing confusion as to why learning any of this was important. How would memorizing the marital affairs of some ancient stranger make my life better? I just didn't understand, and I *had* to find out.

I swung my chair decisively back onto all fours. This was serious.

With genuine interest, I inquisitively raised my hand and asked in only the best way a teenager can, *"Sir, what exactly is the point in learning all this?"* Henry was dead, after all, and I didn't understand how it was going to help me get a job.

The room fell silent as nineteen girls flicked their heads around and stared at me in what looked like disbelief. The mousy-haired girl next to me buried her head in the over-sized issue textbook as if she was embarrassed to even know I existed. It rapidly became apparent that Mr. Burkett didn't like my question. Not one bit.

I was quickly called a *"rude and preposterous little child."* He asked me how I could be so stupid, and I was ordered to leave his classroom until I *"got a brain."* I was humiliated, devastated, angry, and frustrated. I had genuinely wanted to understand the value of his lesson.

Until this point I had been doing well at school despite my repulsion towards it. But this sudden declaration from a *respectable* person of authority—that I was "stupid" and "had no brain"—hit me like a train in the face. Like many young students who have a similar experience, this stimulus turned into a fixed, concrete belief that I was incapable of learning.

My reaction was to withdraw, to hide from my inevitable failure, to give up. I also asked myself *"Why did he respond like that? He's my teacher. It's my job to learn, and his job to teach. If I was a teacher, how would I have answered that?."*

It occurred to me that my response would have been very different if I had been in his shoes. Little did I know that a fire inside me started burning, and that one day it would be an international roaring furnace.

I became obsessed with what a *good* teacher actually looked like, what they did, and how they taught.

I became equally obsessed with understanding how we learn, what engages and disengages us, and what makes the greatest transformational learning interventions.

I soon began a career in the adult education space, with my first post being a Trainer in a male prison in the UK. By the age of 21, I had worked my way up to a Training Manager in the welfare-to-work sector, was well into my degree in education, and was already running my own training organisation on the side that was teaching facilitators of adult learning how to deliver effective and engaging training.

My theoretical and practical experiences combined, and my roles fuelled and informed one another. There began my journey of a life of dedication to contribute to the field of education for the benefit of learner and educator alike.

In my 11+ years of working in the education sector, I have come to learn that it's not *what* is being delivered, it's the *how*. And underneath all of that is the *why*.

After school failed me, I became obsessed with what a 'good' teacher looked like, what they did and how they taught. Now that obsession is leading an industry. What will you change? @CordinerSarah #edupreneur

You CAN make math enchanting. You CAN make compliance training captivating. You CAN engage the disengaged. You CAN make English Literature magical. You CAN make any learning rewarding and transformational.

Learning is NOT boring; bad delivery is boring.

By delivery, I don't just mean the charisma of the Trainer, although that is important. I'm referring to the considerations made to the learning experience during the design of the intervention and, in particular, to the considerations of aligning the training to the principles of adult learning, and that is what this book is about.
I would personally argue that the education we receive, formal or informal, has the greatest influence on our motivations, behaviours, actions, inactions, experiences, careers, relationships, successes, failures and entire life paths, after our childhood years.

If as educators we get this right by embedding the principles and theory of effective adult learning in our formal and informal education programs during the planning process, then we are doing ourselves, our students, and our industry the greatest service by creating and facilitating a platform for success.

So this book is for the conscious edupreneur, the student-centered edupreneur, the edupreneur who sees the value of delivering quality training to their users for long term results and sustainable education-based businesses.

> *"Learning is not boring; bad delivery is boring. Math, literature, compliance training, anything CAN be engaging when delivered effectively"*
> *@CordinerSarah #edupreneur*

This book is less about HOW to build your training courses (as I cover that in my book 'Entrepreneur to Edupreneur'), and instead more about the 'why' behind how to build a training program that is effective.

Understanding the theory and principles of adult learning is the underlying foundation behind all effective adult learning programs. Absorb all that is in this guide, and follow the links to my free resources provided throughout this book, and you will stand out from the crowd as an edupreneur with high quality and transformational training that puts your learners' results first.

This book aims to open your awareness to the many factors that need to be considered BEFORE any training course should be designed, developed, and delivered so that you can be certain that you are creating training that your learners will love. I will take you through the fundamental elements that every adult learning program should include, consider, and cater to, so that your training engages, informs, transforms and creates dedicated lifelong learners who rave about your content.

This book is for the conscious 'Edupreneur' who wants to create and deliver quality training. My training is normally more focussed on the 'how', rather than the 'why', but with an epidemic of bad training practices infecting the education industry as a result of the online learning boom, it is now a critical time to ensure that all well-intended edupreneurs are armed with the must-know principles for creating and delivering quality training. And that means peeling back the marketing hype of 'make passive income by teaching' and instead focussing in on what actually makes a good learning experience, and what the underpinning factors are behind effective curriculum design.

Also, after delivering my online course on 'How to Create Courses' for a while now, I have noticed an increasing number of quality-considerate edupreneurs who enjoy the research, the theory, and the back up as to *why* we construct, plan, and deliver training in certain ways.

It's to keep the standard of education high in a world where so many people are out to make a buck. It's easy to create an online course, which is why the standard of education programs are being rapidly diluted by a lack of knowledge of the principles of adult learning. I wanted to create a resource that would help all conscientious and student-centred edupreneurs get it right, not just for their bank accounts but for the learner's experience, too.

Strip back the online learning boom hyperbole and all the marketing "Make Millions Online" static. This is the timeless *quality education* stuff that underpins all great learning programs, delivered by someone who's postgraduate-qualified in education and has been in the industry since way before it was sexy.

> *Strip back the online learning boom hyperbole to reveal timeless quality training practices @CordinerSarah #edupreneur*

In this book, I present a number of timeless and new age considerations, theories, strategies and principles of formal curriculum design and delivery to enable the modern day edupreneur to be equipped with the most fundamental underpinning of knowledge to develop quality training programs that will serve their learners, their industry and themselves.

THE LEARNING REVOLUTION IS HERE

The education sector has gone from being a formal, unsexy, highly monitored profession to a booming industry that has everyone talking about it and billions of dollars exchanging hands.

The way the human brain consumes and retains information hasn't changed, but based on the social, technological, and environmental influences around us, the way we like to consume that information has. And that means that as non-educational business owners are learning how to educate, whilst the educators are having to learn how to turn their training into something that the world is hungry for, is competitive, and is wrapped in a marketable package.

Education as a profitable business is no longer restricted to registered training organisations, qualified professors, and formal training institutions. With the technology, tools, and apps now available, anyone can create and deliver training for profit from anywhere in the world.

This means that competition is increasing daily for our learners' attention. There is a higher demand for quality content, and there is pressure on how to price within the market yet still make a profit. And there is an ever-present need for educators to become entrepreneurial in order to survive.

As much as the entrepreneur needs to learn how to become an educator, the educator must become entrepreneurial in order to compete. We have a lot to learn from one another.

Combine the expertise of the educator and the entrepreneur, and we have profitable education-based business – or as I like to call it, 'Edupreneurship'.

My next book '*Entrepreneur to Edupreneur*' (available on http://www.sarahcordiner.com/EdupreneurBook) goes into this in much more detail, but edupreneurship is a huge part of the learning revolution. Where there are more learners, there is a bigger need for more training, and the need is increasing every day. However, if the training content we produce, either online or offline, is not considered valuable, helpful, transformational, and engaging, then we won't be around for very long.

Online learning platforms and marketplaces have opened up teaching to anyone who has a desire to share their skills and knowledge @CordinerSarah #edupreneur

What is Edupreneurship?

Essentially, it's educating your market - profitably.

It is the vehicle for initiating and maintaining sustainable business, using the platform of education and training.

It is THE modern day 'tool of the trade' to leverage an organisation's impact, exposure, income AND authority positioning, by educating your market in a profitable manner. It is the new era of doing business. It is the learning (and business) revolution.

It's a platform that you can use to engage, attract, and retain your audience in a way that builds trust AND wins you more business. Importantly, it's about moving away from sales and instead, giving value and information to your audience.

We live in a very different business world now. We cannot just go out there and sell. It doesn't matter how good your website is. It doesn't matter how fancy your business cards or brochures are. Although they are all very important, they are simply not what make sales anymore. Your website doesn't necessarily make people trust you.

Having one doesn't mean that you have demonstrated any kind of credibility that justifies you asking people for money.

It certainly doesn't get you raving, loyal fans. It just makes you another salesperson. Courses ARE the new websites and business cards.

To really get people on board with you—following you, engaging with you, wanting more from you, giving you testimonials about how fantastic you are BEFORE you've even started doing business with them—you HAVE to be using the platform of education. Importantly, you need to be using education *effectively* if you want to get sustainable results for you and your learners.

This means understanding how adults learn, what factors will influence their learning experience, and what considerations and principles need to be taken into account before the designing, developing and delivering processes even begin.

What I am NOT saying is you have to go out and get a degree in education. You are an expert in what YOU do. You are an expert in YOUR industry or particular niche topic, whatever that may be. And that is precisely why you need to be out there sharing what you've got locked up in your amazing brain.

But what we DO need to do, however, is become familiar with the methods required to present your knowledge in a way that your students can easily learn. We need to familiarise ourselves with all of the different ways that your training design can be impacted so that you can plan in advance for it and create training that is ready to transform the life of any learner.

And that's what I'm going to share with you in this book.

Your online course should be so effective that you change your learner's lives. Give them results that will make them your fans forever.
@CordinerSarah #edupreneur

Many people put off writing their own courses because they feel like they don't have enough knowledge. They feel like frauds, or they lack the confidence to pedestal themselves as a thought leader or expert in a particular area.

But you DO have a message.

Think of all the things you know how to do, having learnt them formally and informally. You are literally sitting on a

GOLD MINE of information that people NEED and want to hear, AND want to pay for.

Edupreneurship is different from everyday educational content marketing as it goes beyond just the delivery of information. Thinking, creating and developing educational content like an edupreneur is about identifying where our learners are now, comparing that to where they need to go, and then consciously filling the gaps in a way that will be the most engaging to our unique group of learners.

Moving our learners from one place to another is when we create transformation, and this is the primary goal of every quality edupreneur: to make every person, every life, every business, better than we found it in the first place. It is only TRANSFORMATIVE information that is going to make you stand out from the crowd, which means we need to move from being entrepreneurs to being edupreneurs.

Creating effective training programs requires more than setting up a sales funnel and pumping regurgitated content through it to make money from your customers. It's about changing people's lives with transformational education. Let's learn how.

AVOID THE DARK SIDE OF THE COURSE CREATION INDUSTRY

Ethical, professional, caring and intelligent #edupreneurs know that doing it RIGHT, is doing it best.
Getting money from students comes second.
@CordinerSarah

Having experienced bad teaching in my past that negatively affected my entire academic experience as well as my educational self-efficacy, I am entirely intolerant of bad educational practice, and this is another reason why I have written this book.

Ironically, the very thing I am telling the world to do - teach - is the very thing that I am fighting a battle against.

Teaching used to be considered a qualified profession, and of course it still is. However, with the benefits of freely available and easy-to-use online learning platforms and marketplaces, we are now in a world where anyone can teach. And this is a great thing.

Never before have we been able to share and access skills and knowledge that would otherwise be unavailable or inaccessible. The world is a better place thanks to the fact that we can share and build our skills at the click of a button. It also brings income to hundreds of thousands of edupreneurs who otherwise wouldn't be financially rewarded for their educational contributions to their industries.

I am a huge fan and supporter of edupreneurs sharing their knowledge with the world and doing so in a profitable manner. I dare say I'm one of the world's biggest advocates and drivers of this very practice since I train thousands of edupreneurs every year on how to do it successfully.

However, just like every gold rush, the crooks and the cheats come in with the well-intended crowd. These are the serial online marketers who jump from one sexy trend to the next, never really specialising in anything but pretending to be an expert in everything. They build seductive sales funnels to clean out innocent people of their money until something new and more profitable comes along.

This is where random marketers arrive and offer high-ticket courses to edupreneurs, promising them that they will teach them how to create their own amazing online courses. BUT, they know NOTHING about online course creation, whatsoever. They may have EXPERIENCE in creating their own online courses, but they are not, in any way, educated or trained, or even remotely aware of the fundamental principles of curriculum design and adult learning theory.

Do they make money from their courses? Yep. But do their courses evolve from a design that aims to fundamentally transform the student's life, situation, long-term development? Do they provide an optimum learning experience itself? Are they teaching edupreneurs how to design training programs that deliver the learning outcomes that the learner has paid for in a way that will make them fans forever? Or, are they just telling people to dump a load of content into a learning management system (worse still, an email sequence) simply to pull in some cash?

The majority of these courses I've seen do not. In fact, the only thing they seem to focus on or care about is how much money the instructor will make out of the student, not how much the student will get out of the training.

Although this is great for an initial cash injection, here's the thing: Training that does not transform, does not deliver effective, psychological, sociological, tangible and measurable outcomes and results to a learner, or do so in a way that provides an enjoyable and engaging learning experience, is going to have a lifespan of an ice cube in the Sahara.

The students will come out less than satisfied, won't have anything good to say, and may even have BAD things to say about the course. And after all the love, care and effort you've put in at the direction of these ethicless marketers, you will have an education-based business that will soon be swimming with the fishies, along with your good name.

Scary, right?

So this is another reason that I've written this book.

I have had many course creators come to me having been duped by these industry fakers, and they have come out of expensive training programs with either no course at all, or one that is solely instructor centered. I've had to clean up the mess.

I've also noticed that despite my initial thoughts, there are thousands of online course creators out there who care deeply and passionately about the learner experience. They are far more concerned with what the learner will get from their courses than how much money they are set to make from their students. The ethical, professional, caring and intelligent edupreneur has realised that doing it RIGHT is doing it best.

In 'How To Create Profitable Courses', I have many training videos about adult learning theory and how edupreneurs can ensure that their training meets the principles of adult learning so that their courses are engaging and transformational. I have been pleasantly surprised how many of my students adore these lectures, as I feared so many have been brainwashed about the money.

We've all heard the statistics that the online learning industry is now worth BILLIONS of dollars. This is amazing, but it sadly also means that the education industry is starting to see a flood of unethical Internet marketers, trend-riders and opportunity-grabbers who take advantage of the growing demand of people wanting to learn how to create their own courses.

So, how can we tell the difference between the scammy marketers - who are about as skilled in teaching professional curriculum design as my dog is at doing my accounts - and the course creation educators who are experts in the truest sense?

As you read this book, you will understand that there is far more to creating an online course than throwing together some content and planning a big launch campaign.

'Course Creation' is the sexy new term for 'Curriculum Design and Development', and the latter is a qualified profession from the education industry—not a marketer in his bedroom with a green screen and a 'tried and tested' email sequence.

Most of the marketers out there are failing exponentially to address even the most elementary aspects of curriculum design, let alone consider the needs of adult learners, design a training program that engages and transforms their lives, or leave them with tangible results. Why? Because this bit is not '7-figure sexy' for a start, and secondly, since they are not educationally qualified, most of them don't actually know that there are principles of adult learning and theory to consider when designing effective training programs.

But they are out there, frighteningly making a fortune from edupreneurs like you, but not providing the whole toolbox behind creating truly great courses. So this chapter makes sure you are educated about the differences, so that you can educate others in your entrepreneurial conquests, too.

Two years ago, I paid $25,000 for a program to later find out it didn't exist. I never got what I paid for, and I was refused a refund.

It was a very expensive lesson in doing my research. I always thought that the education industry would be safe from unethical marketers, but I am devastated to find that with the recent boom it has seen, it's turning into a shark tank where hundreds of thousands of edupreneurs (or want-to-be edupreneurs) are being persuaded to hand over their hard-earned cash for subpar training courses on the topic of online course creation. It's going to be devastating to the industry, not only because it risks being tainted with the dirty 'bad marketers' brush, but also because endless reams of bad quality courses will be created as a result, ruining the whole experience for well-intended course creators and their unsatisfied students.

By writing this chapter, I risk getting a million squashed tomatoes thrown at me by big influential marketers, which is why I was too afraid to write it for a long time. But I have been in the education industry for more than a decade, and I refuse to tolerate the unethical practices and scamming that I see happening to my fellow course creators.

They can bring on their tomatoes. I will not allow anyone else to lose their house deposit to an unethical marketer, and although this chapter is a long one, I believe all good-willed course creators deserve this advice, which is why I've included it so early in this book.

In this chapter, I will tell you exactly what to look for and the things you should check before you hand one cent over to someone who claims they can teach you quality course creation or conduct curriculum design services for you.

So what's wrong out there?

- Marketers create their own overpriced and inefficient courseware website plugins and then claim to be able to teach you how to create courses so they can sell you their software.
- Random solopreneurs say "I made a course once, so

I can teach you how to be an educator."
- Experts seem to have no particular expertise whatsoever, other than jumping from selling the nuts off of one hot trend to another over the years. They claim that because THEY have created and sold online courses, they are now qualified to teach curriculum design.

That's like me saying "I'm a dentist because I know how to brush my teeth."

Just because I have brushed my teeth for thirty years, and have perfect white pearlies to show for it, does NOT mean that I am qualified to go about acting like I'm a dentist and getting my hands stuck in YOUR gnashers. And would you even want me to?

Yes, the internet marketer who sells you his or her "amazing thousand dollar online course training program" may have a GREAT track record of making money from their own online courses in the past (or so they tell you). But often their claimed success is in direct correlation to their ability to conduct successful marketing and manipulate buyers into trusting them and handing over their hard-earned money - NOT their ability to design training programs that meet the principles of quality curriculum design and effective adult learning.

"*But I took his/her marketers course and I liked it.*" Maybe, but are you a qualified curriculum developer? If you don't know what the correct form should look like, how would you know if it was missing?

I get clients coming to me who have been *ripped off* of thousands of dollars by these industry boom surfers. They have been fooled by the marketing hype and shouty '*Buy My Stuff Now'* webinars, and then they come to me deflated, exhausted, broke and upset to get the mess fixed up.

Do your research before you pay 'expert' course developers.

Educational curriculum design and teacher training is a *qualified profession*. It is an industry in its own right and encompasses a lot more than just 'throwing a bunch of research together' into a Word document.

Let's just put this into perspective.

You wouldn't get surgery from an unqualified doctor. You wouldn't get a building designed by an unqualified architect. Do not get your courses, your IP, and reputation designed by unqualified curriculum developers, and do not get 'teacher trained' by unqualified educators!

If you don't check for this, don't *expect* your course to come back with any degree of quality, and certainly don't expect your IP and reputation to be constructed in a way that's going to bring you any long-term credibility and value.

Don't get scammed, my fellow course creators. This is your IP, your business, your credibility, your money and your reputation we are talking about.

If you want to learn how to create engaging, transformational and profitable training, there are lots of qualified course creation experts out there with brilliant programs who can help.

> *Educational curriculum design and teacher training is a QUALIFIED PROFESSION. Throwing some research into videos does not make a course*

@CordinerSarah #edupreneur

To avoid any risk of giving your hard-earned money to the wrong person, make sure you check the following nine course creation scam warning signs:

They will tell you that you won't need to do any research.

I saw a recent advert for a Create Your Own Online Course program by an unqualified course creation marketer who said that if you use their method to create an online course, you won't have to do any market research as they had a 'shortcut' to check if you have a marketable product. WHAT?!!!!!

Stop what you are doing and listen up.

If *anyone* tells you that you can create a quality, marketable *anything* without doing research, then RUN AWAY AS FAST AS YOU CAN.

Any *true* professional will tell you that no matter how much you think you know your market, extensive market research is absolutely CRITICAL if you want to actually sell anything, let alone something people will like. Creating online courses is absolutely no different.

Yes, research is hard work and a bit boring, but you want to sell your course and have people love it, don't you?

They are not qualified educators or curriculum developers.

Check for qualifications to ensure they have the technical skills to design quality training. Curriculum developers and/or your teacher trainers should have a DEGREE in education at the minimum, and at LEAST five years proven experience developing and delivering training to accredited standards. That is if you want to be taught how to develop quality training programs.

I'm not saying you have to be a qualified teacher to teach a course, NO. I'm saying you have to be a qualified teacher to teach teacher training because it's a qualified profession. I'm not saying you have to be a qualified curriculum developer to write a course, NO. I'm saying you should be a qualified curriculum developer to teach curriculum design/course creation. Make sense?

They have no historical background in the education industry, curriculum design and teacher training.

Check for history in the marketplace to ensure they're not a new industry 'trend-hopper', just jumping into the industry to make a buck. Check all of their social media, their websites, their LinkedIn profiles. Understand how long they have actually been teaching 'teacher training' and course creation (curriculum design). And I don't mean the length of time that they have been creating their own courses. Remember brushing your teeth doesn't make you a dentist and doing home reno's doesn't make you a registered builder. I mean, how long have they been TEACHING CURRICULUM DESIGN? If you cannot find substantial historical evidence of their dedication to this profession, you may want to question if it is indeed their profession.

Look towards the professionals who were in the industry long before it was sexy and profitable. You know those people are in it for the love, not your money.

They have no proof of their expertise in using national training frameworks and meeting regulatory standards in education design.

Check that they have proof that they have developed compliance-approved training to Qualification Framework criteria to ensure that they can produce to regulatory body standards. They should know what national training frameworks are and who your local regulatory bodies in training compliance are. They should be able to tell you what the principles, regulations, conditions and requirements of formal adult education programs must look like, and what they must adhere to. If they can't, may I suggest that they are lacking in the basic expertise required to create quality training.

They are charging you for access to a Facebook group

Really?! If an online program has been designed according to adult learning principles, then you shouldn't need to go to a Facebook group to seek your course support, feedback, advice and communications about your course progress. There should be in-course discussion areas and constant opportunity to get direct feedback from your course teacher. Isn't this what you're paying for?

If I paid an 'expert' for access to a course, I would expect to get their expert advice, not be palmed off onto a Facebook group where it's expected that the community will help me. If you look at this offer from the eyes of an educator instead of a marketer, the learning community should be an intrinsic part of the learning process, not a substitute for teaching or another income stream for the 'admin'.

There are literally THOUSANDS of Facebook groups out there, all free and pretty much filled with all the same people anyway. I have one that not only shares valuable learning DAILY, it's FREE. You can join for free here: www.sarahcordiner.com/FacebookGroup

You don't need to pay extra to be part of a community of like-minded people. Why should you be charged to access something that is not costing the supplier anything? If they convince you that you cannot do without this Facebook group as part of your course, then you should question the thoroughness of the course.

They put high pressure on you to buy NOW.

In one breath, they'll tell you that having an online course is the ultimate way to scale your business (true), but then they'll say things like "*There are limited spaces*," or "*Hurry up before the spots run out.*" (Hypocritical much?!) Get real.

This is the internet. The reason course creation makes for a scalable business is because there is no maximum capacity, and in reality, we course sellers want as many people to buy as possible.

By using this scarcity approach, marketers force us to make rapid decisions, often leaving us wondering what happened when we see our bank account a few days later. If you're being pressured to buy an online product RIGHT NOW (which can't actually 'run out'), then think twice before you buy.

They tell you that if you get it wrong, you're ruined.

I recently saw an advert for an online course creation program that said if you get lost in your course creation then it will be impossible for you to recover, and it reinforced that it's something that you MUST get right the first time.

Rubbish. We all get lost, stuck, overwhelmed and paralysed by stuff in our businesses every day, yet we still get through it. We all stuff up from time to time, yet we are still around and probably a better businessperson for our stuff-ups. We all look back at our first drafts of stuff we built, designed, went to market with, and we absolutely cringe at the memory. Remember your first website?! First drafts don't make you fail!! First drafts are PROGRESS.

My first courses SUCKED, and still to this day, I am rewriting, adding to and updating my courses because the world constantly changes and that means that a great online course is never truly finished. Don't be believe that you have to get it right the first time or 'you're ruined'. This fear mongering is another marketing tactic to subtly force you into buying their product. It's cruel, and it's wrong. Please don't buy into it.

They tell you that you couldn't possibly do it without them.

Short of doing myself out of work here, I have to say that is complete codswallop, too. Think of all of the things you know how to do today that you didn't know how to do five years ago. Humans have an unparalleled ability to learn new things, and with the array of information out there, believe me when I say that there is NOTHING that you can't teach yourself. Yes, it will take you a LOT longer than getting a professional to teach you. Yes, you will make a lot more mistakes and do things the slow and hard way when teaching yourself. Yes, it won't qualify you in anything, but the point I'm making is that you can still go out there on your own and create a course.

So when you see the "You're too stupid to do it without me" marketing tactic being used with the intent to overwhelm and frighten you, remember that you do have a brain and that you should think very carefully about giving your money to this person.

They don't show you the curriculum in the sales process.

Now THIS is a big one! They will make a HUGE sales page going on about a load of vague idealistic outcomes you'll experience by buying their course. For example, passive income, scalable business, private memberships, magic blueprints that have no explanation. They'll claim that you'll be implementing these and getting your hands dirty. But they don't tell you HOW. They only show you part of the curriculum ... blah blah blah.

Where is the full list of lessons you're going to get? Where are the learning outcomes? Learning outcomes, when written PROPERLY are clearly defined and have MEASURABLE results, not cloudy promises of a 'six-figure passive income business'. Not that there is anything wrong with that – IF they actually deliver it.

EVERY course MUST have a full, detailed curriculum plan that clearly outlines every single piece of content, learning outcome, and lesson that will be taught. If one of these does not exist, the course has not been properly constructed by an 'expert' course creator. It would be like building a house without the blueprints.

In my bad experience, I did not see a written curriculum outline. I paid for a program to later find out that it didn't exist. If you don't know what you are buying or if you can't see the FULL itemised description, then please ask yourself what you are paying for!

Many marketers use the "*Sell It Before You've Built It*" technique. This means they get YOU to pay them for something that doesn't yet exist. All well and good if they actually do build something to give you, but as an experienced course creator, I can confidently tell you that a program usually evolves as you build it. Therefore, it doesn't always end up identical to the original course plan, the one they promised you.

If you are buying ANY kind of training, course or coaching program, ask to see the FULL curriculum, as well as a sample of content from throughout the program (not just the first module) *before* you hand over one cent so that you know it actually exists. A list of every module title and lecture title, and a short selection from each lecture is enough for you to know that there is a product ready for you to access the second you press the 'Pay Now' button. If a provider has a course ready to go that they are proud of and passionate about teaching (over just making money), she will be delighted to do this for you.

Show your full curriculum outline and have free samples of your course - you'll make a lot more sales when people know what they are buying. @CordinerSarah #edupreneur

They have no historical content or IP on course creation, teacher training or curriculum design.

Someone who is TRULY invested in their area of expertise will have dedicated hours upon hours upon hours to their art.

- Do they have a website or a blog? Does their blog contain substantial content demonstrating their expertise in the topic; in this case, online course creation and curriculum design?
- Do they have a YouTube channel? Does it contain substantial videos that demonstrate their expertise in course creation?
- Are they sought after as an expert in course creation? Have they published articles? Are they sought after to be a keynote speaker? Have they been interviewed on podcasts? Do they have a book or ebook on course creation?

If someone is trying to convince you that they are an expert in course creation yet they have not bothered to take the time to establish themselves as such by topic content creation, I would be inclined to believe that they were jumping on a trend to make money, rather than being a dedicated professional in that topic.

In conclusion

Before you give your money to a expert course creator to learn how to build your course, or one that will design your course for you, remember that professional expertise goes far beyond being able to sell a topic well.

It takes YEARS of working, living and breathing that industry. It requires formal and informal training and years of practical experience and content curation in that topic. I know. I've been doing this for over a decade, and it kills me to watch innocent course creators trying to better themselves for their business and their students getting hurt. Check this stuff out first.

REALITY CHECK: ARE YOU READY FOR TEACHING ONLINE?

When you create a course that's popular, you must be ready to deal with crazies, critics, and the rewards of many happy students @CordinerSarah #edupreneur

The second you take your training off the hard drive and onto the internet, you immediately open up a global marketplace for yourself. This brings with it mind blowing opportunities. The number of people you can help becomes limitless without you having to do any extra work.

You can increase your profit margins. Once your course content is filmed and the initial start up expenses are paid, every sale is 100% profit thereafter. Dare I say it? You also become a little famous in your industry area. People can now find you and see your skills in action from their own screens, when previously you would have been invisible to them.

This is when you wake up to messages from complete strangers from all over the world thanking you for changing their lives and helping them make their dreams come true. The feeling is incomparable.

However, there is also a dark side that comes with the bright side. And the brighter the sun is shining, the darker the shadow it casts.

Get Ready for 'The Crazies'

You will attract people who absolutely adore you when you start creating great courses. Some may love you a bit too much. You will also attract some people, by default, who don't like you at all. There can be all kinds of reasons, and usually the majority of them are things that you really can't do much about.

I've had people complain that they don't like my accent, or the way I look. I was hilariously told I "*look like a Barbie doll drone*" by one of my students! Short of putting on a fake accent or having a face transplant, there's not a lot I can do about this kind of feedback, and so I have to learn to ignore it.

I had a reader become extremely offended when I rather thoughtlessly used the word *Jesus* in one of my videos. I even had a student complain that I talked about myself too much in the 3 minute '*About the Trainer'* video!

I've even had a competitor log into my courses just to leave rotten reviews, then request a refund on their way out. In short, you WILL get haters - people who are crazier than a bag of intergalactic space rabbits - and people who will get spitefully critical of your personal looks or perspectives. It's just the nature of the playing field.

You don't have to be *okay* with it, but please go into online course creation with a willingness to accept that it's part of the job. Make yourself not get too caught up in 'negative Nellies', unless it is a constructive opportunity to improve your program.

The Hard Knock of the Bad Review

Next, there is the public review process to deal with. I've had clients create their first course and feel utterly crushed when they get a bad review or a refund request, and they are usually the toughest-shelled creatures.

The difference between going online and being in the physical classroom is that the risk to our reputation, and dare I say it, our egos increases dramatically. In the traditional classroom, bad reviews are restricted to a feedback form that often is shoved in a drawer somewhere, never to see the light of day again—at least not by anyone other than the Trainer. However, the online feedback is posted on a public page for the world to see, and this can impact future sales.

Freeloaders can often use this fact to their advantage and get your content for free. Twice in my eleven years, I've had customers send me private messages and threaten me that "if you don't give me a full refund, I am going to destroy your name online." One person who did this particularly well was a lady I will call *Tacy*. She sent a barrage of hate mail to me asking for a refund, threatening to 'tear me down' online if I didn't. I gave her a refund because, well, she was utterly insane – and she still went out and bad-mouthed me anyway, whilst re-enrolling in three of my other online courses and going back into the *same* course she asked for a refund on in the first place and left a five-star review! Yep. You will get all kinds of bizarre experiences the more successful your courses become, and you need to be prepared for this, even EXPECT it to happen, before you embark on your journey.

You need to make sure that you read each piece of feedback with one thing in mind: *"Can I use this to improve my courses?"*

If the feedback does not help you do that, simply ignore it. Make sure your energy goes into those people who DO love your content, which is going to be almost all of them.

Are you ready for this? It's never nice, but as time goes by, you do learn to become more neutral to these realities of online course creation.

It's Not a Guarantee to Wealth.

Finally, another must-know reality check is that this might not make you rich. Too many course creators only read the marketing hype about online course creation. They rush off to create an online course thinking about the colour of the Ferrari they are going to buy. Then get really upset and angry when their launch is comprised of crickets and tumbleweeds.

In my book *Entrepreneur to Edupreneur,* I go into the commercial side of course creation and education-based business building in far more detail, but in short, please know upfront that creating a course is only the beginning. You need to have a well-planned out business model and at least an 18-month marketing plan to support a successful course. You cannot just "build it and think they will come."

Your course sales will be directly proportionate to the amount of effort you put in. If you do nothing once your course is built, you won't make any sales. If you are not prepared to work hard for a long time, then this is not the right business for you.

I hope I haven't scared you off! I really debated whether to put this section at the beginning or the end of the book, but I decided that readers deserve to know the truth and have the reality check right at the beginning.

This chapter isn't to frighten you or put you off the incredible journey of becoming an edupreneur. It's to open your eyes to the reality of this booming industry right from the outset. This book isn't just about how great it is to build something that will changes people's lives and make yours better in the process, too. It's about informing you of the highs and the possible pitfalls so that you can be empowered and in charge of your edupreneurial ventures for years to come.

Being a course creator is one of the most exciting, rewarding and enjoyable experiences in the world. I hope that by sharing these warning signs with you, I can help ensure that your course creation and online teaching journey is nothing but a wonderful one as you go about spreading your message, creating your legacy and changing the world.

If you are still here, let's learn how to plan for effective adult learning, shall we?

EFFICACIOUS EDUCATION

In my opinion, ensuring that education is efficacious is hands down the most important part of designing and delivering effective adult education programs.

So what is efficacious education?

'The Efficacy Effect' is a concept I have termed that illustrates how and to what extent people can influence results through their belief in their ability to control various life events. Our everyday experiences - indeed, our entire life path - can be influenced by our perceived ability or inability to succeed in any given activity, despite what our actual ability may be.

Apply this to the educational context and our sense of self-efficacy in the 'classroom' can have a monumental impact on our academic or personal development achievements. Our existing belief systems, and subsequent behaviour patterns, have been sculpted via an array of influences.

These can include your own evaluation of your past successes and failures, watching others who are similar to you succeed or fail, things people have said to you, your emotions and your personal characteristics.

These perceptions are the result of our experiences, environment, culture, and social groups, and they often exclude a factual analysis of our real abilities. Consequently, many of us make major life decisions based on false interpretation, misguided mindsets about our ability, and delusional concepts of our (non)competence to achieve.

"*Everybody is a genius,*" said Albert Einstein. "*But if you judge a fish by its ability to climb a tree, it will live its whole life believing that it is stupid.*"

Many of us face this kind of crushing judgment. We accept it as truth, and allow it to shape our lives. Not anymore!

This chapter aims to show the edupreneur one of the most powerful ingredients possible that you can add to your training.

Understanding and applying techniques in your training to increase your students' educational efficacy will make you a better leader, parent, friend, educator or self-motivator. I also hope it will show you how a tiny action can cause a reaction great enough to change the life course of even the toughest-shelled human.

Unlock your learner's educational efficacy. It changes their motivations, actions, careers, relationships and entire life paths. @CordinerSarah #edupreneur

'Efficacious' comes from the Latin word 'efficere', which means 'to accomplish'. Essentially, it means being successful in achieving a desired result or outcome. Efficacious education therefore means achieving desired results in the educational setting, but with the development of learner self-efficacy at the core.

To have 'self-efficacy' is to have faith in your ability to achieve your desired results. In education and training, I believe that building learning that delivers results, and builds our learners sense of their own self-efficacy, is one of the most powerful and transformational outcomes our training can ever give.

Let's go back to my history class, shall we? So there I was in the UK in summer 1994, packing up my little Garfield pencil tin, stuffing my oversized history textbook into my navy rucksack, and sorrily shuffling out of the classroom wondering what on earth had just happened. "Don't come back until you've got a brain, Sarah." When would that be? I wondered.

Here is the part of the story that I haven't told you yet, the most important part for you as an educator to understand. After my horrible history teacher had diagnosed me as "not having a brain" for asking the andragogical question "What's the point of this class, sir?"—things really took a turn for the worse.

Like many young students who have had a similar experience, this stimulus turned into a fixed, concrete belief that I was incapable of learning. My reaction was to withdraw, to hide from my inevitable failure, to give up. And I did.

I soon noticed that teachers began teaching me differently. Even when I COPIED my friends' homework word for word, they got 'A' grades and I got 'C's. How could this be? It's the phenomenon of the reaction theory in the '*Educational Efficacy Effect*' at play.

Sarah Cordiner

I was ignored when I asked questions, and teachers asked me to go clean out lost property boxes instead of join the class. These insults were the last straw for my efficacy. All my hope of being anything or anyone vanished. I resigned myself to being a failure. All that was left was to wait for the day I would finally be free from the misery and oppression of education.

I often asked myself, "Why did he respond like that? He's my teacher. It's my job to learn, and his job to teach. If I was a teacher, how would I have answered that?"

It was at this point that I began to take refuge in the art classroom. Since it was clear that my academic teachers didn't care if I was in their classes, I was soon skipping most of them to immerse myself in a form of expression that had no right or wrong, no boundary of correctness or benchmark for assessment.

I found a place where I could be alive and safe from failure. It was there, in that art room, that a mentor crossed my path and changed my life forever.

He gave me a gift - precious, powerful and immeasurably potent with positive force. It is the reason why I am alive today. Well, happy and successful. Two years had passed since my educational efficacy had been turned on its head.

My art teacher had now become my only cheering supporter. He showed me, a young woman who had entirely given up on believing she was capable of learning, that I had in fact made monumental achievements. He had been aware the whole time, even though I had not been, that I had been completing enough pieces of art to pass my A-Level exam. He secretly invited an art gallery to see my work. The gallery commissioned me to create a solo exhibition and informed me that the art invigilator had paid a generous amount of money for two of my paintings.

I was absolutely blown away. Was this what success felt like?

I was elated, and totally taken aback to know that I was a person capable of achieving it.

My art teacher showed me that I was indeed brimming with competence, ability and talent. More importantly, he showed me that learning, succeeding and achieving involved more than just memorising the names of promiscuous royal gentlemen or the chemical equation for photosynthesis. He showed me that learning and success took many different forms.

This simple revelation, his encouragement and reminder that I had already proven that I could achieve, gave me the confidence to retake all the exams I had previously failed.

With his constant reminder of my ability to create desired results, I faced my limiting beliefs, my fears, and the ridicule. In just twelve months, I passed all eleven of my failed exams with exceptional results. My realisation of the power of efficacy was born.

As soon as I realised that I WAS capable, that I could achieve, that success is something that was attainable for me, my educational and professional motivation went through the roof.

I started setting goals, and my aspirations grew from my own survival to being the greatest version of myself so that I could help other people discover their own efficacy.

> You CAN change the WORLD when you design and develop training that truly has the efficacy of your students in mind.

@CordinerSarah #edupreneur

My newfound efficacy also inspired me to show that horrible history teacher how he should have answered my question all those years ago.

From that moment, I was motivated by a burning desire to pass on the miraculous gift of self-efficacy that my art teacher had so generously given me. I had experienced the best and the worst of teaching, and it had taught me a LOT. I became obsessed with what a good teacher actually looked like, what they did and how they taught.

I became equally obsessed with understanding how we learn, what engages and disengages us, and what makes the greatest transformational learning interventions.

Thus began my journey of dedicating my life to contributing to the field of education for the benefit of learner and educator alike.

Today, my business has educated thousands of people in over 120 countries, and it changes lives every single day. I continue to create desired results, both personal and professional, through building a belief system based on one's ability to achieve—all thanks to the singular intervention of one humble man who cared enough about ALL of his students' lives to make a difference.

Today, I thank my appalling history teacher for teaching me how not to teach.

If only I had my history teacher's email address....

Here's how my history teacher could have answered my question many years ago:

"Sarah, everything we are experiencing today is a result of what we did yesterday. You can spend today waiting for tomorrow to be great, or you can spend today creating greatness, so that tomorrow will give greatness to the world.

You are the author of your own destiny. You have the power to write your own future, and therefore your own history. Today is the first day of the rest of your life. Take it and ensure you are the best 'you' you can be. That is what this history lesson is all about."

Sadly, he didn't say that, but my art teacher found a way of allowing me to figure it out for myself. I have now dedicated my life to passing that message on to others in every way possible.

The moral of the story?

Efficacy is the greatest influence on our motivations, behaviours, actions, inactions, daily experiences, careers, relationships, successes, failures and entire life paths.

One tiny event can be received as a life-changing shift in mindset, which creates a reaction in proportion to that person's experience. This reaction is experienced or witnessed by others who can add to the mindset, negatively or positively by their own reactions. And so a pattern begins to emerge.

Teachers, trainers, educators, leaders, coaches and parents are ideally positioned to be Efficacy Effectors. Get it wrong, and you're the horrible history teacher who will ruin potentially magnificent and successful futures. Get it right, and you will create a butterfly effect of success stories and wonder in every life you touch.

This chapter is dedicated to helping you do just that.

The power of efficacy, hey? It still blows my mind that the development of efficacy—or 'efficacious education' as I have termed it—is not a part of many school curricula, and I am gob smacked that it is not even mentioned in many course creation training programs since it is so fundamental to student success, both in the training and afterwards.

If your online or offline training programs embed efficacy as one of the fundamental outcomes of your training courses, you will leave a true legacy behind you. You will leave students feeling confident in their abilities, who believe they are capable of achieving their goals, and who are motivated to go and get them. This is true educational leadership in its most actualised form.

This is how good people change the world for the better. I do this in as many ways as I can, which I will explain later, but I have one driving core value:

How can I make this world a better place than I left it?

Yes, I said WORLD. You CAN change the WORLD when you design and develop training that truly has the efficacy of your students in mind.

All you have to do is break it down to "How can I leave each individual person better than I found them?" And before you know it, you've indirectly impacted millions of people.

When your students acquire self-efficacy in your topic, they often go on to do great things with the knowledge and skill that you taught them, and many go on to teach others, too. Those people then go on to teach others, and soon, you have a domino effect, or rather an Efficacy Effect, of change made in the world, all of which were sourced from you and your student-centered training.

One of the biggest compliments I get from my students and my community members is that they feel I deeply care about them, that they KNOW I believe in them, that my teaching encourages them to take action and always gives them results. As much as I hate to say this, this doesn't necessarily happen because I have the best courses in the world. It's because as I teach and communicate with my audience, I strive to make them see and feel that THEY are the best students in the world—that THEY are immensely capable, skilled and oozing with brilliance in their own unique ways.

I don't strive to do what marketers teach you and make the training design all about making myself look like the smartest person in the room. I strive to make my students feel like they are the smartest in the room in their own fields, as this is part of what builds an individual's self-efficacy.

Before we go any further into the methods you can use to build your students' efficacy in your training, let's have a closer look at what efficacious education looks like in comparison to general education:

General educational outcomes could include:

- Achieving learning outcomes
- Acquisition of new skills, knowledge and competencies
- Development of employability, personal and professional skills and knowledge
- Development of desired attitudes and behaviours
- Development of transferable skills and knowledge
- Development of own ideas and concepts

Efficacious Education includes all of the above AND the following:

- Development of a positive sense of self, self worth, self confidence and self-efficacy in the learner
- A sense of confidence in trying their hands at new tasks and activities
- A sense of belief in their ability to succeed in achieving a desired result in the learning environment, task or activity
- A sense of knowing that they are capable of independently executing what has been taught
- A feeling of confidence about their skills and

> knowledge in the topic so that they could go on and teach it to others

-

Interestingly on this last point, I often say when I deliver my Course Creation Bootcamps that my main role is to provide such a thorough schedule of training combined with embedded development of self-efficacy for my students that I will essentially be redundant by the end of my boot camps. They simply will not need me ever again.

I also see a number of my own students go on to create training programs that attempt to compete with mine. They contain replications of my training content and materials. I am yet to be offended in any way by this as I, in fact, feel the opposite. I cannot be a trainer of trainers—the global leader of edupreneurship— and expect to NOT create versions of myself. That is my entire objective—to see physical evidence that my training has given so much skill and efficacy to my learners that they feel able to go on to teach it themselves. This fills me with utter pride and purpose and is the key to my mission of making the world a better place.

By building up my own students' efficacy, I am achieving exactly that. In early 2015, I set myself a 5-year goal to educate 10,000 edupreneurs by 2020. But by 2016, I had already educated 6,000, and so I upped my goal to educate 10 million people by 2020. I NEED other edupreneurs to help me on my mission to make education better for everyone.

ACTIVITY: Thinking About Efficacy

What is your dream for your students to achieve, do and be by the time they finish your courses?

_____

_____

What do you want them to feel empowered to achieve?

_____

_____

I consider the self-efficacy element as the most important part of course creation. Without the inner belief that they have the ability to achieve desired outcomes, our students are less likely to take educational risks, which is fundamental to their personal, professional and academic success.

Going back to my own story, I believe that there are far too many stories like mine. Almost every single day I hear from adults who remember negative educational experiences. This is detrimental not only to their continued education in adulthood, but as previously mentioned, it can also impact their lives on a much greater scale.

Like a self-fulfilling prophecy, one simple stimulus can go on to affect our thoughts, behaviours, actions, inactions and life outcomes because of the way it made us feel and think about our ability to achieve desired results.

Let me explain this further using my model 'The Efficacy Effect'. This model is explained further in my book *The EFF Word*.

THE EFFICACY EFFECT MODEL

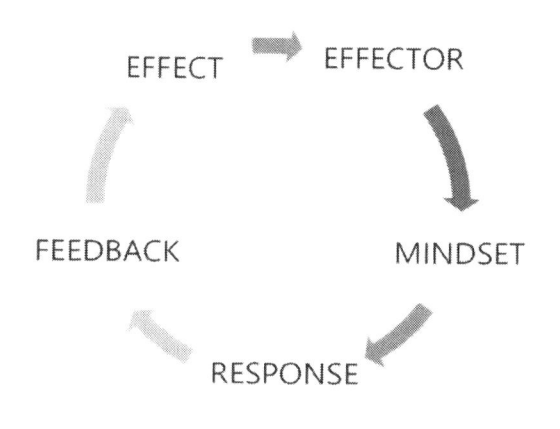

EFFECT → EFFECTOR

MINDSET

RESPONSE

FEEDBACK

Model by Sarah Cordiner ©

The Effector

An 'Effector' is any event, experience or stimulus that impacts the way we think or feel about ourselves and our abilities to achieve desired results. These events or experiences can be both positive and negative as the cycle goes both ways.

One tiny educational event—a teacher telling you that you are stupid, failing a test, or not understanding a teacher's explanation—can instigate a life-changing shift in the way you perceive yourself and your abilities.

Either way, this trigger causes a new thought process. As edupreneurs, it is important that we realise just how powerful everything we do and say can be to our students and their subsequent success.

How we address our students, give them feedback, evaluate their work and respond to their questions all act as Effectors, which can instigate a positive or negative imprint on their self-efficacy in your topic.

Mindset

The 'Mindset' part of our model refers to how our thinking is altered by the Effector.

All of us react differently to the events and experiences we have in our lives. Some of us are more resilient than others, and some of us simply care about different things, including the opinions of others. However when the event or experience (the Effector) impacts something that is important to us, it becomes significant.

A seemingly meaningless experience becomes something that can ultimately affect our future thought processes and behaviours to similar experiences in the future.

For example, if we are told we are stupid enough times, or by someone with authority or whose opinion we take seriously, then it is highly likely that we will begin to actually believe that we are stupid.

In summary, the mindset phase is when the Effector affects us to the point to which it changes, influences or impacts the way we think and feel about our competence, abilities and chances of success regarding the topic in question.

Response

The 'Response' part of the model refers to how we react to the Effector. Once we experience an Effector that shifts our mindset and how we think and feel about a situation, it then affects our behaviour. Our behaviour is so heavily determined by the way that we think that the mindset becomes the driver of our actions and reactions to what we have experienced.

Going back to my story, being *told* I was stupid made me *believe* that I was stupid (the mindset). This caused me to react and withdraw from my education (the behavioural response). By seeing myself as incapable of academic success, I retreated from it entirely. I bunked off school. I stopped going to classes, and I dreaded any form of formal learning because I believed that I was incapable of succeeding.

This is a clear example of how the Effector can influence our mindset, which then goes on to affect our behaviour. How easily this can happen to your students, too.

Feedback

This stage happens when our reaction to the Effector is experienced or witnessed by others who can further reinforce the experience by what *they* say or do in response to the behaviour they observe coming from us.

Here is an example to make this easier to understand:

Effector: Imagine a child in school is told by a teacher that he is not very good at math.

Mindset: He sees the teacher as an authority so believes what the teacher says, and now he thinks he is bad at math.

Response: Because he *thinks* he is bad at math, his natural instinct is to withdraw and switch off from math. After all, why invest yourself in something at which you think you will not succeed at?

Feedback: Everyone notices his lack of application in math class, and because he is no longer engaging, he falls behind. People start treating him as someone who is not very good at math. The teacher doesn't bother trying to engage him anymore. He is left to sit in the corner and do nothing each lesson. Because people are treating him this way, it not only reinforces his new belief that he is not very good at math, but now he starts to make the belief even more powerful because this so called 'information' is now actualising in real life.

Since we as humans generally place a heavy value on what other people think, say or do towards us, this can often be the cementing point of a self-fulfilling prophecy.

The feedback stage's power is often grossly underestimated in the educational environment. As soon as the reactions and behaviours of others start to reinforce the initial positive or negative Effector, the sooner the situation, thought process and behaviours of the individual are justified, inciting the "I told you so" mentality.

Effect

The final stage of the efficacy effect model is the effect stage.

The effect is the overall result of the entire experience. It is the holistic amalgamation of the thoughts, feelings, attitudes and subsequent behaviours that we have because of the original effector.

We are essentially a new kind of person when we get to this stage, as the combination of the Effector, the new beliefs, our subsequent reactions and the reinforcing reactions of others now forms a new reality, a new lens through which we see our world and our place within it.

In the above example of a child in math class, the final effect will be a boy who has actually become an underperformer in math. All from a simple statement from a teacher.

And so a pattern begins to emerge.

We see this pattern clearly in delinquent behaviour. During my time mentoring for the Devon Youth Offending Team and whilst conducting my teaching practice in a UK prison, I got a real insight into why many of my highly intelligent, exceptionally skilled learners found themselves incarcerated in the first place. Many of them told me stories that all began the same way: *"At school my teachers always used to tell me off and put me in 'time out'. I was never good at school. I always failed my tests. My teachers told me I'd never amount to anything, so what was the point in bothering? I was always getting told off when I didn't do anything wrong, so in the end I thought that I might as well just do the things they were telling me off for, because they were already convinced I'd done it anyway."* Interesting, isn't it?

If we say someone is naughty enough times, the efficacy effect model tells us that a prophetic pattern will emerge so that eventually, that individual will begin to act naughty. If we tell someone that they are clever, smart and competent, they will feel more efficacious about learning new things and apply themselves fully to achieving in an educational environment.

When it comes to the educational setting, thoughts, feelings, behaviours and attitudes develop that are either opposed to lifelong learning or accepting of it.

That is how efficacious education is formed.

So as you can see, the power of influence we have over our learners—whether they are children, adolescents or adults—is absolutely huge.

I believe that effective adult learning programs require the facilitator to be fully aware of the efficacy effect and how critical it is for us to design and deliver training that creates desired results, not just from a learning objectives point of view but from a place of fostering an environment of efficacious education.

Understanding how adult learning principles apply to your training design and delivery is pivotal in helping Effectors push learning experiences into the realm of positive effects.

Teachers, trainers, educators, thought leaders, learning and development managers, training organisations and coaches are ideally positioned to influence the learning cycle. Get it wrong, and you're the horrible history teacher who will ruin potentially magnificent and successful futures. Get it right, and you will create a butterfly effect of success stories and wonder in every life you touch.

Getting it right will also benefit your retention rates, feedback, referrals, and results if you're the facilitator of the learning in some capacity.

The simple difference between the two is that bad learning interventions do not incorporate the principles of adult learning, but good ones do. It's essential that anyone involved in the design and delivery of training and education understand how adult learning principles work.

This all starts with us understanding the adult learner.

> *Embed adult learning. Bad learning interventions do not embed the principles of adult learning. Good ones do.*

@CordinerSarah #edupreneur

Theorists such as Malcolm Knowles tell us that adults learn in very different ways from children.

A combination of current life situations, past experiences and learners' reasons or motivations for being in the learning program can all influence how much an adult will take from a learning experience, as well as their attitude and approach to education altogether.

In this book, we explore some of the theoretical concepts of adult learning to better understand the adult learner, their needs and whether there are better ways that we can facilitate positive transformation in our adult learning interventions.

Although this book does not explore an exhaustive list of adult learning frameworks, I encourage you to consider ways in which the various theories and models that are discussed relate to your own experiences and observations, both as a lifelong learner and as a contributor to the facilitation of adult education. Such analysis brings continuous improvements to the learning processes within your field.

BUILDING EDUCATIONAL EFFICACY

If we want to have a successful online training program, we need to design and deliver our training in a way that creates successful students. Whether you are teaching a highly technical topic like computer programming, or an obviously heart-centred program such as mindfulness, you are ALWAYS teaching confidence, self-esteem and self-efficacy. If we choose to ignore this, then we are choosing to ignore our own success, too.

When a learner has high self-efficacy about your topic, they are more intrinsically motivated to complete your course and apply your lessons. Therefore, they are much more likely to get the results you designed your program to give in the first place. If you are supporting their efficacy as you teach your course, they see the challenging elements of your training as an opportunity, instead of a threatening experience to be avoided.

According to Albert Bandura, a significant researcher in self-efficacy, there are four major ways that we can increase our learners' self-efficacy in our training programs:

1. Mastery Experiences

This is the most powerful efficacy influencer of all. When we experience 'mastery', we are learning from our experiences. If we fail at something, our sense of efficacy in that subject will decrease. If we experience success from our educational efforts however, we will be encouraged and motivated by similar situations in the future. By creating learning experiences that allow our students to frequently taste success from their efforts, we will be increasing their motivation and efficacy in the topic.

2. Vicarious Experience

When we watch someone else succeed in a topic, we are experiencing vicarious success. If we can see that other people are successful, it makes us feel safer, and as such are more likely to expect to succeed in that experience, too. Therefore getting your students to share their progress, wins and results is a great way to show new learners that they can get the same results if they follow the steps you have prepared in the training.

3. Verbal Encouragement

Just as a negative comment can decrease self-efficacy, positive comments, when said with conviction, genuineness and credibility, can boost a learner's efficacy. Providing positive, factual feedback about their progress can work really well here.

4. Influencing Mood

The way you present your content can affect your learners' self-efficacy. Excitement, enthusiasm and happiness are all contagious emotions that can increase the feeling of efficacy. If you are nervous as you teach or if you are talking with a stern, authoritarian voice, you can cause the learners to feel nervous for you or intimidated by your practice, which will increase their anxiety and negatively impact on their efficacy. Pay attention to the learning environment that your own mood and delivery style are creating. If you worry about your teaching, you can be assured that your learners will worry about their learning.

Here are 12 other ways that you can increase educational efficacy for your students' success:

The Way You Respond, Communicate and Connect

This requires a careful balancing act. Our students come to us for our expertise and advice. This often makes course creators feel like they have to go above and beyond in interactions with their learners to make sure that they look like the genius expert they think their students expect them to be. To look smart, they give long, complicated answers, or they blind their learners with technical jargon. But ironically, if we respond to their requests for help in a way that makes them feel like they are less than us, less intelligent than us or have less worth than us, we will actually hurt their educational experience and even our relationship with them. We must ensure that we are paying careful attention to the WAY that we respond to our learners so that we provide them with the information that they seek in a way that is not self-glorifying, over-complicated or patronising.

Create a Collaborative Learning Environment

Although we will go more into creating positive learning environments in a later chapter, a study by Fencl and Scheel showed that a "collaborative learning and the use of electronic applications showed a positive correlation with increased self-efficacy in their student sample." The same study also showed that question and answer, conceptual problems and inquiry lab activities as teaching methods also increased learner self-efficacy.

Do Not Compare Students to Each Other

Everyone learns at their own pace, so what might be a huge step forward for one student could be a miniscule progression for another. A sure way to make the majority of the class lose their educational efficacy is to compare them to the ones who are doing well. This method will certainly help the top performers gain a hefty dose of efficacy, but it ostracises and demeans all other students. The comparison method, no matter how it is done, will always have losers regardless of how intelligent they are collectively. Instead, it is much better to use an ipsative approach to assessment if this fits your type of educational program. This means assessing students from their own starting point.

One method that I use to do this is to create Likert Scale assessments that are statements formed from the learning objectives of the course. The students read each statement and rate themselves on a scale one to five as to how much they agree with or are like that statement at the beginning of the course. They then complete the same assessment at the end. This will show a quantifiable measure of their progress. I found that this method works well when collecting data about training programs whose effectiveness is traditionally harder to measure.

For example, I teach confidence and motivation programs for single mothers, which is often federally funded. Naturally, the government likes to have data on the effectiveness of our programs to ensure there is value for the money spent. But this topic is very hard to collect proof that development has taken place. I also teach business development programs for franchise businesses, and the franchisors like to ensure that their franchisees are getting a return on their investment in my training.

Often the success of a business is restrictively measured by whether or not it makes more profit during the year that the training took place, which isn't always representative of the acquisition of critical skills and knowledge.

You can use the following ipsative assessment method in formal and informal training settings (online and offline) to gather highly valuable quantifiable data for your various stakeholders regarding the effectiveness of your training. I use this method and accredited assessments to gather the personal development progression information, as well as the academic progression.

Here is an example of how I use this method in our Entrepreneur Business Development Training Program:

Sample of Learning Outcomes:

- Develop clearly defined company visions, missions and values
- Identify practices and systems in your business that are causing inefficiencies
- Identify the most effective strategies for growing your business in the next twelve months
- Identify and implement at least five online tools and or apps that will increase productivity in the business
- Develop a clearly defined strategic plan for the business for the next twelve months

Sample of the Ipsative Assessment:

Learners will complete this at the beginning and the end of their training to ascertain their progression from their own starting point, but not as a comparison to their peers. This increases self-efficacy substantially, as there is *only* progression. They cannot go 'backwards'. They cannot fail, and there is not a benchmark of what is good or bad. There is only a visual marker of where they are at the end compared to when they started, and if your training is designed to provide the outcomes that it promised, then progression should be guaranteed. Go to www.sarahcordiner.com/precourse to view a real example of an ipsative assessment.

Balance the Challenge and the Wins

Your training should be hard enough for your learners to feel a true sense of victory when they complete it, but not so hard that it makes them feel incompetent. You also want to make sure the little wins come often, but that your training is not so easy that it is condescending to their intelligence.

This involves knowing who is in your target audience, their previous experience level in your topic, and how advanced they want and need your training to go. It may also require in-depth market research if you are designing a non-accredited training program, and careful attention must be paid to any hidden or specified prerequisites in an accredited training program.

If students get 'free wins' from simple, non-challenging tasks, it does not increase their self-efficacy at all. In fact, it can even decrease efficacy because the feeling of 'fraud' can come from getting wins from tasks considered too easy. Therefore, it is important for us to provide small challenges throughout our training, so that learners have the opportunity to feel a true sense of achievement by overcoming something that wasn't easy.

If it were all hard, they would give up. If it were all easy, they'd feel like the program was a waste of time. Adding interspersed moments of easy wins with challenges is a great way to get learners engaged, with a constant opportunity to feel their abilities shifting as they progress through the program.

Include Cooperative Learning in Your Courses

A study by Albert Bandura also showed that in learning experiences where learners work together, help each other and communicate as a team on educational activities, their educational efficacy increased in comparison to situations where learners worked on individual or competitive educational projects. This could be due to the fact that when students work in a non-competitive manner, they see how they are similar (even better) than their partner, rather than being forced by the nature of competitive situations to see where they lack in comparison to those they are working against.

In the online course realm, there are many ways that you can encourage cooperative learning—discussions, online communities, and local and/or remote groups. With forums, video conferencing, Skype, facetime, livestreams and more now easily and freely available, it's not difficult to get learners from all corners of the globe working collaboratively in your training programs.

Create Clearly Defined Short-term Goals

A fundamental human need is to feel we have a sense of control over our circumstances, and this comes from being able to predict and prepare for where we are going, what we are doing and how we will do it. The more prepared and in control of their learning, the more likely your learners will feel confident, motivated and efficacious about attaining the outcomes that have been set. This observation is backed by Schunck and Pajares who suggest that setting short-term goals, that are challenging yet attainable, will help increase the efficacy of our learners.

Get Learners to Verbally Report On Their Own Progress

Sometimes when we are busy in the throes of daily life, we can have our eyes so close to the road that we cannot see just how far along it we have travelled. We can feel like we are not progressing when in fact we have made significant progress.

When we stop to intentionally take stock of where we have been and where we are now, and then verbalise that progress with others, it reinforces our success and subsequently increases our efficacy and sense of ability to achieve that task. In your online courses, have regular check-stops where you get learners to share their progress with the rest of the group. This can be done through a discussion feature, a share in a social media group, or a 'round robin' in a live webinar. All of these can work really well for this.

Avoid Rigid Teaching Techniques

When a learner is being taken through an online program that has a very rigid, inflexible delivery, it can be easy for them to get lost and drop out of the learning. For example, if the training goes in specific steps with a 'must follow precisely' methodology, when they are stuck at one single stage, they will remain stuck there if there are no alternative development or completion pathways.

As an example in my online course, '*How to Create Profitable Courses*', in the section about structuring your content in your online course, I present at least four methods that all vary in application and complexity that can be used to structure a course. If I taught one single method and a learner was to get stuck at that stage, they would be very likely to remain stuck there and not progress beyond that point in the course. By providing multiple ways around this stage, I have given the flexibility for all different types of learning preferences, styles and abilities to succeed in overcoming the challenge of that module, thus increasing the chance of efficacy in course creation for all of my learners.

Don't Make it Too Flexible

Just as we don't want to be too rigid, we also do not want completely loose and undefined methodologies. Just like how having too many shopping choices in a supermarket can cause 'buyers paralysis', when learners have a limitless option of pathways, tools, strategies and choices, their brains can quite literally freeze. They don't know which way to go. A simple lack of decision-making, caused by too many choices, can be detrimental to efficacy.

Play on Their Passions

People are always better and more successful at things that they are passionate about. It's obvious that if we enjoy something, all challenges will feel far less intimidating than the same level of challenges that come from something we dislike.

If we design our training to allow our learners to bring their passions, hobbies and interests into their learning then we will significantly increase efficacy in our training programs.

If they love something, it means that they are already familiar with it, feel empowered by it and enjoy it. If we can combine the most challenging parts of our training with the learners' passions, we will see less resistance, higher efficacy and greater completion rates in our courses.

Give Them Power

This aligns somewhat to the self-directed principle of adult learning, as well as to the concept that we are happier when we feel in control. If you can allow your learners to have some degree of influence over their learning program, their feeling of control with give them efficacy, as they will choose the pathways where they feel most comfortable.

For example, this could include allowing them to choose from three different ways of being assessed, such as a multiple-choice test, a written essay or a project submission. They could choose whether they work on a project alone or in a group. You could allow them to decide if they will study part time or full time. There is no limit to how you could apply this concept in your training courses. As long as you find a way to give your learners a taste of control over their learning, they will increase their educational efficacy in your course.

Assign 'Failure' Appropriately

Failure is not a word I like to use in education; as although we can 'fail' a test, that 'failure' is a result of the measures of competence that are being used, not necessarily a lack of development in the student. Failing a test does not mean that learning has not occurred. However, for the purposes of explaining this concept, I will use the familiar term 'failure'.

If a learner is underperforming or fails in your training program, their self-efficacy will immediately drop because they feel as though they are incompetent. You can reduce the risk of a negative 'efficacy effect' initiating at this stage by communicating with the learner that the failure is due to a lack of action or implementation, not incompetence or "stupidity."

People don't internalise failure when they can attribute it to simply not doing something. However, if they feel like they are flawed in terms of intelligence or skill, their efficacy and motivation will suffer.

ACTIVITY: What Will Your Learners Be Efficacious About?

In what do you want them to feel totally competent?

_____

_____

At what do you want your learners to feel successful?

_____

_____

List the top three things that you will do in the design and delivery of your training programs to ensure your learners leave your training with increased self-efficacy.

_____

_____

_____

_____

INFORMING YOUR PRACTISE WITH THE THEORY OF ADULT LEARNING

Children and adults learn differently. Children learn well with a didactic approach to teaching (teacher dictating and telling), whereas adults require a much more complex array of considerations made to the training design and delivery in order for it to be effective.

The process of engaging adult learners in a learning experience is known as andragogy. The term was originally used by Alexander Kapp, a German educator, in 1833. Later it was developed into a well-known theory of adult education by the educator Malcolm Knowles who arguably stands as one of the most influential writers in this field.

Knowles (1984) distinguishes adult learning from the pedagogical approach of child learning in a number of theoretical ways. In this book, we will explore how these theoretical concepts of adult learning apply to the way we design and develop our training programs and facilitate the learning experience.

It is believed that children actually take on the components of an adult learner between the ages of twelve to fifteen years old. Therefore, variations of these principles of adult learning have become prevalent talking points in the development of training and curricula in recent years. They are increasingly used in the goals of schools, colleges, training organisations, universities and, slowly, businesses to enable their students and staff to become effective lifelong learners.

Sarah Cordiner

In order for adults to learn effectively, training needs to be designed in a way that meets the following core principles of adult learning:

1. Self-directing
2. Learn by doing
3. Relevance and readiness
4. Experience
5. All of the senses
6. Practise
7. Personal development

In the following chapters, we will go into each one in a little more detail, with some tips and strategies to help you embed each principle into your training programs.

> *Adult learners need to know what the training program is going to give them and what their life will be like at the end*

#edupreneur @CordinerSarah

THE PRINCIPLE OF SELF-DIRECTION

Adult learners like to be self-directing when it comes to their learning.

In essence, self-directed learning is about enabling a learner to move from needing a teacher to help them achieve the outcome of the course, to being able to autonomously and independently achieve the outcomes without supervision or coaching. This should be the aim of every online or offline course creator and educator.

Does your course create independent practitioners in your topic? If the answer is yes, you already have a course foundation in place that has a self-directed approach. Luckily, this very principle of adult learning lends itself perfectly to online learning, as it is extremely self-directed in nature. The learner usually discovers the course through their own search efforts, makes an independent choice to enroll, and then fits the learning into their schedule as it suits them.

DIY education is the number one way that most post-compulsory education adults learn in the modern world. This means that having online courses that facilitate meaningful self-directed learning journeys have exceptional value.

However, good self-directed learning offers more than simply 'leaving them to it.' If we want our learners to get the most from our training programs, we need to add some conscious facilitation to our curriculum planning process.

Know What 'Need' You Are Meeting

Self-directed learning is active learning. Adult learners consciously select and engage with content that they find useful and have an immediate need for. They reject or ignore content, which they feel they already possess or don't need.

When this active problem-centered approach to learning is facilitated, it can significantly enhance the learning experience. Our training will be more interesting and desirable for our learners if they can apply it to their own needs. By default, it increases the sign-up rate to our courses as well because people buy solutions to their problems.

Reinforce the Results Your Course Produces

Results, results, results! Adult learners need to know what the training program is going to give them and what their life will be like at the end of the course.

First, ensure that you have conducted market research to ascertain the precise results your audience is looking for. Then you can use this research to enhance your sales copy and your learning outcomes so that you can paint the perfect tangible picture of what their life will look like by the time they have finished your course.

It also optimises the amount of information our learners will retain. When they have decided for themselves that the training is of value, importance and relevance to their immediate needs, they can better encode, conceptualise, synthesise and remember what is being taught.

Know Their Laws and Values

Adult learners self-govern, and they live unto their own laws, beliefs and values. If adult learners feel that you are driven by different reasons or want different outcomes, they will be less likely to engage in your training.

For example, some people are highly driven by financial outcomes, and therefore they will be the types of student who will engage in training that helps them achieve a certain financial result. Whereas other people are completely turned off by financial goals and would prefer a course that focusses on an affective or emotional result.

When you know what your students stand for and you design your training to enable them to apply it in a way that meets their own values, you will be facilitating another element of self-directedness in your courses.

Give Them Control

We need to design our training programs in a way that allows for a degree of learner independence. Whereas children feel safer when they are taught didactically (meaning dictated to or told what to do), adults need to feel they have more control over the learning experience.

Malcolm Knowles, the godfather of adult education theory, describes self-directed learning as "*a process in which individuals take initiative without the help of others.*"

The common image of teaching and learning is an individual going to a teacher, or someone more experienced or knowledgeable than they, to be "instructed to." Although this is what happens in literal terms, the (happy) adult learner usually considers themselves in charge of the situation.

According to Knowles' adult learning theory, THEY sought out the learning opportunity, THEY initiated it, and THEY are responsible for finishing it as well. So design elements of your training that involve you taking a controlled and designed step back, and giving them the reins where appropriate.

Tell Them Why

Adult learners need to know and understand the exact benefits and purposes of the learning program. If adult learners cannot appreciate the purpose or the value of your course, then they will be reluctant to engage in your learning program.

Present Clear Learning Outcomes

Adult learners like to diagnose their own learning needs and formulate their own goals. They then select and engage in the training programs that they feel are best going to meet those needs and goals.

Therefore, having explicit, clear learning outcomes are critical for the adult learner to make decisions as to whether your course is right for them. If they cannot see how your course is aligned to their own self-imposed objectives or how it will help them achieve those objectives, they won't buy your course.

Enable Self-enrollment and Flexible Start Dates

Adult learners like to feel as though they are in control of their own learning journey and that it's all under their own terms.

They have to take on the primary responsibility for the planning, the initiating and even the conducting of the learning project itself.

Ensure that your courses have a self-enrollment function where possible so that they can start whenever they want, log in whenever they want and pace themselves as they want. Of course, this may not be an appropriate feature for more date-restricted synchronistic training, however it's worth considering adding this flexibility.

Give Them Challenges

Since adult learners will only voluntarily enroll in courses that promise the solution to a problem, we can increase their self-directed experience by giving them solution-focussed challenges as part of the learning process.

Student self-efficacy increases when they are given tasks that challenge them enough for success to taste sweet, but not so hard that the fear of failure is stressful. Motivation increases when it is obvious that the result will help them achieve their goals, which is why they took the course in the first place.

Ensure They Can Monitor Their Progress

The great thing about adult learning is that we don't have exams to pass or fail. This is unlike our formal education, which many of us don't remember fondly. For the adult learner, success is measured in very different ways. Specifically, they must see how far they have come from their own starting point and how close they are to reaching their personal goal.

In the 'DIY' self-study adult education world, our learners no longer sit on a scoreboard with a class of similarly aged and experienced peers. We are on an independent journey, and we cannot compare our experiences to the experiences of our fellow students. Therefore, adult learners are only racing against themselves.

If your course can include a way that they can quantifiably measure their own starting point and reassess themselves throughout the learning journey, then they can clearly see how they are travelling along their own syllabus.

I use what is called ipsative assessment for this, especially in my training programs that have more qualitative data such as feelings. Also, they want to know what their progress is in the overall completion of the course. Ensure that the entire curriculum is clearly laid out so that they always know where they are on the map. Even if your course is drip fed, they must know exactly what is coming next so that they can track how they are travelling.

As a tip, success breeds success. Therefore, a bundle of shorter courses will drive more results and higher completion rates than one big course.

Allow Them to Work in Their Preferred 'Zone'

Some people prefer to write on paper with coloured pens and sticky notes. Some prefer digital work. Some like to watch videos, while others prefer PowerPoint slides that they can print and doodle on. Some like to listen to audiotapes on the way to work, and others like to discuss their work in social media groups or face-to-face.

Design your training to allow self-directed learners to pick how they learn. Ensure you have flexible learning methodologies so that although the same principles, skills or knowledge are being taught to your learners, they can encode and practice in their own learning preferences or processing styles.

For example, in my course How to Create Profitable Courses, I teach my learners how to structure their course modules. I actually present them with a number of methods that they can use to structure their course so that all learners can pick the methodology that best suits their learning preferences and natural working styles, instead of being dictated by my own biased approach.

> *If learners cannot see how your course is aligned to their own self-imposed objectives, they won't buy your course.*

#edupreneur @CordinerSarah

EMBRACE INDIVIDUALITY

When planning our training design, we must also check that we are not painting all of our learners with the same brush, assuming all learners are the same. Knowles' theory of self-directedness that states most adult learners like to feel that they have a degree of control over what they are learning is true, but we must not assume that all adult learners are highly motivated to learn.

Since the majority of adult education is not compulsory, the learner's willing and voluntary involvement in the learning program is higher than that found in compulsory education. In fact, as such, it would support an active compliance from learners. We must remember that compliance does not necessarily mean positive or productive learning activity. In our role as the developers and deliverers of the training, we must do so in ways that fuel engagement.

Compliance and engagement in learning programs is heavily dependent on individuals and their unique motivations for engaging in the education. Flaws in the self-directed concept of adult education are pointed out by the likes of Smith (1996), who notices "*the point at which a person becomes an adult, according to Knowles, psychologically, is that point at which he perceives himself to be wholly self-directing. And at that point he also experiences a deep need to be perceived by others as being self-directing*" (Knowles 1984, p.29).

Both Erikson and Piaget (1982) have argued that there are some elements of self-directedness in children's learning too (Brookfield 1986). Children are not dependent learners all of the time. Learning for them is an activity that is natural and spontaneous. (Tennant, 1988. p46)

From my experience as an adult learner, I have found that it can sometimes be difficult to stay focused and motivated when embarking on self-directed projects. Not all adult learners are naturally self-motivating. So, we must be sure that we have ways of ensuring that the benefits of completion are valued by the learner and that we are monitoring and encouraging progress throughout, and after their learning journey.

An autonomous approach alone could easily allow failure to occur, which is why we should avoid totally self-directed learning, such as wholly online learning courses that have zero facilitation, interaction or guidance from a 'real' human, if we want to instigate true transformation. If our aim is simply to deliver information, the purely autonomous approach is sufficient, but we can expect retention and completion rates to be lower than with those programs that deliver mixed methodologies and engagement strategies.

You can add some teacher-led elements to training that is mostly self-directed with a blended learning approach, such as adding live webinars or workshops and group work (in person or remotely via video conferencing). You could also use automation software to track progress made in the online learning environment and send automated emails with content that is in alignment with their progress on the course (or lack of it).

REFLECTION

- Has there ever been a time that you or your organisation developed or delivered training in a way that assumes all learners are the same?

- How can you ensure that the most independent learners have the freedom they crave, whilst the more dependent learners are given sufficient guidance?

- What could you add to your online course system to provide more guidance?

THE MISTAKE OF OVER-INDEPENDENCE

As Knowles tells us, we must ensure our training programs allow our students to be autonomous in their learning.

However, in some instances our attempt to give students independence actually leaves them feeling isolated and disengaged.

This is when the '*teacher*' needs to become the '*facilitator*' to avoid isolation and to give enough freedom.

A simple lack of decision-making ability, caused by too many choices, can be detrimental to learner efficacy. #edupreneur @CordinerSarah

Teaching is when we impart our knowledge to our learners, whereas *facilitation* is when the educator creates a learning environment that allows the learners to feel like they've done the work themselves. The facilitator guides the process but does not contribute opinion or content with explicit answers, thus encouraging the learners to find it for themselves.

The likes of Merriam (2007) would suggest that in the independent pursuit of learning, educators are required to assist individuals or groups of learners in locating resources or mastering alternative learning strategies, not in providing it on a plate.

The learners themselves are encouraged to seek out their own assistance, perhaps in learning communities, peer-learning environments or through learning technologies. The facilitator simply checks in on their progress at set review points.

An example of this may be a man doing some DIY on his house. He may refer to a book, a magazine or the internet for technical information. He may ask a builder friend or the staff at the DIY shop for advice. Before starting, he may speak to friends that have already completed this activity on their house. This approach is self-directed in essence, but requires the interactions, guidance and input from others to be successful. Therefore, it is not learning in isolation.

A more personal example would be my attempts to write this book for instance. It is a form of independent study. I have been on a self-directed (autonomous) educational journey that has required me to look at a number of pieces of work relevant to this field, acquire and read books, and ask colleagues and other experts for their contributions and feedback. Without involving these outside influences in the process, my learning would have been slow, and it would be a lot less likely that you would be reading this book!

REFLECTION

- In what ways do your teaching practices embrace and support self-directedness through facilitation, over teaching?
-
- What other methodologies and practices could you use to support your learners' autonomous learning

journey whilst minimising the risk of isolation?

The Summary of Self-directedness:

Whether you call it self-instruction, self-education, independent study, self-learning or self-directed learning, this principle of adult learning places our role as adult educators as the metaphorical lighthouse that guides our students as they steer their own educational ship.

Create training that allows your students to enroll when and how they like, to engage with your content when and how they like, to apply your theory into their own practice in their own way, and to feel as though they are responsible for their own practical and theoretical success as they progress through your training program – yet do it in a way that does not leave them isolated and alone.

> *Adult learners like to be self-directing when it comes to their learning. Let them lead their learning journey.*

#edupreneur @CordinerSarah

THE PRINCIPLE OF MOTIVATION IN LEARNING

The next concept of adult education we will look at is one of the elements of andragogy that was added later. This principle is about the motivations of adult learners, and it is an important factor in how much they engage in education or learn from it.

In addition to some of the approaches to adult education highlighted in the previous chapters, Lieb (1991) suggests that there are six general sources of adult motivation to learn – or reasons underlying their enrollment in your course. Figuring out what these are for your learners will help you make more sales if you bring in references to these motivations in your sales copy, and will increase enjoyment and retention rates if you design your training around attaining the these motivational results for your learners as well as the key outcomes.

Learner motivations for enrollment could include:

1. Social relationships: to make new friends
2. External expectations: to fulfill the expectations or recommendations of someone else
3. Social welfare: to improve ability to serve mankind, prepare for service to the community, and improve ability to participate in community work.
4. Personal advancement: to achieve higher status in a job, secure professional advancement, and stay ahead of

Sarah Cordiner

competitors.
5. Escape/Stimulation: to relieve boredom, provide a break in the routine of home or work, and provide a contrast to the monotony of everyday life.
6. Cognitive interest: to learn for the sake of learning, seek knowledge for its own sake, and satisfy an inquiring mind.

As adults, our motivations for learning vary due to different environments, different times of day, different topics and even the different food we have been eating. It would also be inappropriate to assume that all adults have the same motivations for embarking on a learning experience, but the above suggestions by Lieb do act as a useful framework for consideration.

As we will shortly see, there are a number of ways to increase a learner's motivation to engage in training programs, but we can start quite simply by reinforcing the benefits to be gained in each of the six areas listed above.

ACTIVITY: YOUR COURSE MOTIVATORS

Think about your target learners, their circumstances, needs, desires and fears, and list everything that they will gain or avoid by joining your course. Then consider how you will ensure this is embedded into the course design, delivery and even your course sales copy.

List at least 3 ways that you will provide each of the following to your learners:

1. Social relationships

2. External expectations

3. Social welfare

4. Personal advancement

5. Escape/Stimulation

Sarah Cordiner

6. Cognitive interest

Educational researcher and theorist Jurgen Haberman suggests that there are three main reasons why adults learn, in addition to the list of motivators above:

1. Work
2. Relationships
3. Emancipatory action (freedom from restraint)

It was later suggested by Mezirow that as a result of these three main reasons for adults to learn, the most important task for adult educators is to help adult learners become more aware that the way they see themselves, other people and the world around them is affected and influenced by their psychocultural assumptions. Psychocultural assumptions are the way they think and behave in group situations in reaction to their physical and environmental surroundings, and their personality.

In simpler terms, Mezirow is suggesting that as adult educators we must embed learning into our training programs in a way that encourages the learner to think about and consider their own attitudes, stereotypes and assumptions about a topic, context or subject area.

ACTIVITY: ADDRESS EXISTING ATTITUDES

1. What pre-existing attitudes, stereotypes and assumptions are your learners likely to have about your topic before they start your course?

2. How will these affect their learning experiences if you do not address them?

3. How will these affect their learning experience if you do address them?

4. How can you design your training program so that your learners will think deeply about their preexisting

   - attitudes?
   - stereotypes?
   - assumptions?

Finally, as we continue to explore how we can better design and deliver our training programs to trigger and enhance the motivation to learn within our learners, here are six strategies that we can use, suggested by adult and continuing education professor Stephen Brookfield.

1. Ensure there is a voluntary participation in learning.

One of the great things about teaching in the post-compulsory sector of education is that most learners engage voluntarily. When learners *want* to learn, this makes for a much smoother educational process. However, in the case of some workplace learning, welfare-sector training and prison education, I can say from significant personal experience that learners frequently have no choice. They *must* enroll. In these circumstances more than ever, the course creator and facilitator must ensure that they have planned the training in a way that will enhance the participant's motivation to learn – so that after the first session, they continue to come back willingly.

2. Promote, provide and show mutual respect.

I would argue that this is a human right more than an educational principle. Our learners want to be respected as much as we do, and so managing our classroom, virtual or physical, needs to be done in a way that ensures our learners feel equal to us. Check your language for condescending connotations, your physical position looking down or up at them (on screen or in person), and if you are sharing or dictating when speaking.

3. Encourage a collaborative and community spirit.

There is significant research that shows that learning is enhanced when it occurs in a network or community. Even Maslow's hierarchy of needs shows us that a sense of belonging is critical to survival. If you can design your training to make your learners feel like they belong to something, that they and their circumstances are similar to others, and that they matter, you will certainly enhance the learning experience for them. Facilitate an environment (virtual or physical) where our learners feel comfortable asking each other for help and advice, where they work together, collaborate and build friendships outside of the formal learning schedule.

4. Ensure there is structured allocation of time for action and reflection.

True transformation only happens when learners have had the opportunity to implement strategies that will move them from point A to point B. Ensure that you have designed specific opportunities and scheduled time for doing and implementing what they have learned in your training. As they progress through the training, the more tangible results you can get for your learners, the higher their motivation and overall appraisal of the training is likely to be.

5. Provide critical reflection and ensure learners conduct this in their own learning.

Reflection is a powerful learning methodology in adult education, so much so that later in this book I have dedicated an entire chapter to it. This is about creating much deeper cognitive, affective and perceptual transformations in your learners by facilitating reflective learning in your program. This is about getting them to look retrospectively and from different viewpoints at their topic, and consider their progression through it in a way that can provoke learning beyond the scope of the curriculum.

6. Ensure there is significant opportunity for self-direction.

As already covered in an earlier chapter, adult learners hate to feel controlled, manipulated or stifled by anyone or anything else. The more we can allow for individual influence and self-directed learning opportunities in our training programs, the more motivated our learners will feel to continue engaging in it.

STRATEGIES FOR MOTIVATING AND ENGAGING THE DISENGAGED

I have shared how I started my teaching career designing and developing training programs for the long-term unemployed in the welfare to work sector, as well as in the prison education system. In these situations, the majority of my learners were sent to me without a choice and were highly disengaged from learning. Many of them had awful, if any, memories of education - memories of failure and humiliation, or simply utter boredom at the thought of it. Their motivation often exasperated further due to a lack of literacy skills that left them behind right from the outset of any past education.

Similarly, as told earlier in this book I was also a student who hated school, thanks to my horrible history teacher whose unprofessional actions instigated a limited educational efficacy in me.

In addition to the strategies described in the last chapter, there are further methods that you should consider if you are working with those who are disengaged in the learning process. You should factor in how you will embed such strategies throughout the training design process.

From my experiences, one of the key things I have noticed when it comes to learner motivation is how they feel about their ability to be successful in the given topic, particularly those who are less motivated. Yes, it's that old educational efficacy thing again.

If you were being forced to play a game that you felt you couldn't possibly win, how would you feel about having to play the game? Even if you were highly cooperative and did what was asked, you would feel drained, despondent and that your time was being wasted.

Often, educational programs and educators themselves (cue my horrible history teacher) actually cause educational disengagement. They use activities, tests and language that actually highlight the students weaknesses rather than celebrating and building upon their strengths. This further crushes any ounce of self-efficacy a student may have had in that topic as the very act of failing the test, or not knowing the answer when they were put on the spot, or getting the demo wrong reinforces their existing sense of "*I can't do this.*"

I am not saying that we should ignore our students' weaknesses. No, our very function is to help students get better at everything.

But, we need to be critical about HOW we are making students aware of their strengths and weaknesses, and provide them with an equal balance of challenges and wins.

Training and developing people is supposed to facilitate change and provide a positive experience, a successful outcome and better lives for the participants. Yet change is a phenomenon that often generates fear, resistance and heel dragging. Let's face it. The very essence of education is change. We are attempting to change thoughts, knowledge, skills, perceptions, as well as attitudes, behaviours, and much more. This can generate resistance, often from our learners' fear of the unknown. If we are to design and deliver effective training programs, we need to make sure that we are aware of all of the ways that training can affect our learners' motivations and put into place various strategies for keeping them invested in the learning process.

To ensure a successful learning and development program, it is vital that change-makers, leaders and educators of all kinds know how to apply the top three techniques for engaging reluctant participants.

The need for personal control

Humans have always tried to exert control over their lives to gain favourable circumstances and avoid unfavourable ones. This has been the blueprint for our survival.

In Greek mythology, the story of the evil king Sisyphus illustrates how having no control over one's life is considered a greater torture than hell itself. Sisyphus's punishment for being an 'evil' king was to keep pushing a huge boulder up a mountain, only for it to always roll back down again – forever. The reason this was seen as a great punishment, is because the sense of helplessness caused by the feeling of no control or progress, is quite literally torture if experienced enough.

As soon as change causes us to feel like we're losing control over our current and future experiences, we naturally resist. We run away from the change, drag our heels, sabotage it, or go into outright rebellion against it, for our own protection.

Having a sense of control over our circumstances by being able to predict them and plan how we will manage them provides two vital benefits:

1. It gives us confidence that we are facing a non-threatening experience that we don't need to resist, and

    2. It ensures a greater likelihood of a desirable outcome to that situation (because we can plan for it).

Change, especially when initiated by someone else, brings uncertainty and distress. This stems from the feeling that we have lost control, and our ability to predict, plan and prepare for change is diminished.

When it comes to our learning and development initiatives, we need to do the following to counter these feelings:

1. Remove the fear

When an unsuspecting employee is suddenly informed they have been enrolled in a training and development initiative, they may assume that it's because they're not good enough at their job, which naturally generates defensiveness and resistance. If a welfare dependent suddenly is enrolled in a course they know little about or have limited motivation for, then they will not be able to see how it is a worthy exchange of their time. When people don't know what is going on or why, fear of the unknown becomes a major barrier to learning.

To prevent these kinds of disasters, here is one of the many techniques I have in my toolbox, which you're free to use immediately:

- Ensure that you appraise the motivation of the participant before the training/development program. Doing this not only shows your informed commitment to their development, but provides a platform from which to initiate a consultation based on the recognition of skill, contribution and further potential, instead of an identification of weaknesses.

- In the pre-program appraisal, highlight their strengths and achievements. Use explicit examples to tell them what they have done well and what the business has gained from their contribution, if they are employed. This verbal affirmation is a source of efficacy for the individual, which is the single greatest motivator for an individual to take positive action and achieve desired results in their lives. If you cannot identify any achievements or contributions the learner has made to something (an existing or old job role, a group, another learning experience), I would strongly suggest revisiting, or developing a thorough personal or professional development plan. There is a simple template for a personal development plan for free at www.sarahcordiner.com/pdp.

- Explain to them how you intend to use training and development as a way to move their skills and contributions to the next level.

- Use positive language (e.g. you wish to *build* on their strengths), not negative (they need to be upskilled to fill gaps).

- Finally, now that you've increased their efficacy and willingness to undertake training, engage them further by demonstrating the need for it. If the training/development initiative is aimed at employees, explain the vital skills that are required to meet the next 1-5 year strategic business objectives. Tell them that you see them being a part of that. If they are not employed, you can look at the industry they wish to be part of, and research and predict the needs of that industry in the coming years. Then discuss how they would like to grow with it. According to Maslow, people can only perform at their best when they have a sense of belonging and identity. Explaining where they fit into the long-term plan provides this. It also gives a reason to make the intervention a success. In short, clearly explain their purpose, relevance and identified role in the long-term result of the change.

2. Allow them to plan

Predictability is vital to humans. It allows us to prepare mentally, emotionally, and physically; plan what we will say and do; and determine what resources and experience we will require; and so on. This gives us a sense of control over the situation. Perceiving that we have no control or influence over a situation generates worry, distress and dispiritedness.

As a leader, educator or instigator of the training/development initiative, it's important for you to recognise that participants who feel they can plan, prepare for and shape a meaningful outcome are more likely to participate.

Consult with the participants about the training and development initiative as much as possible.

- For learners you cannot meet in person, you might create an online pre-course survey, using tools such as Google Forms.

- You can further assist in your learner's planning and preparedness by using a thorough and systematic enrollment system. The system should provide chronological detail of what will happen, what will be expected of them, what they can expect in return, the benefits to them, and so on.

- Somewhere in this process, be sure to give participants an opportunity to ask or express what they want to get from the training and development initiative. What new knowledge, skills, mindset, attitude, or experience would they love to walk away with?

As well as the formal pre-enrollment procedures, at the start of any course, I always ask my learners to write down their hopes for the program.

If you are delivering your training face to face, you can accomplish this by doing a verbal round robin, or even getting them to write their hopes on posters on the walls. If you are delivering your training online, you can simply add a discussion board or a poll in this section near the beginning. This is a great way to get everyone engaged and bring a sense of belonging and community.

This helps me find ways to embed the additional hopes and expectations into my training and add further value for the participants. I let the students know when I have embedded an additional element into the training to make them aware of their contribution to the experience.

I always revisit these hopes at the end of the training to ensure that all the planned and additional hopes and outcomes were fulfilled. When this happens, nobody walks away feeling like they've had a negative or pointless experience.

3. Remind them of the relevance

Training and development that is highly relevant to a participant ensures higher engagement, motivation, contribution, retention and completion rates.

We reject what we deem irrelevant. As discussed, Knowle's theory of andragogy says that all new learning must offer immediate relevance to our lives for us to deem it worthy of our time, commitment and brain capacity. If your participants consider the training irrelevant to them or their lives, they will be unmotivated, disengaged or even rebellious towards it.

To solve this, contextualisation is the key. We cover this in more detail later, but here is a brief overview of its application in terms of motivation.

Contextualisation and Motivation

1. In your description of the training, outline why and how it will be useful to each participant's life, job role, future, and so on.

2. During the training, consistently emphasise how every skill, nugget of theory, and example is applicable to every person, job role, and the business and industry they belong to.

3. If you are conducting employee training, ask the client for a copy of their 1-5 year strategic company objectives (or at least a condensed version), participants' resumes and a copy of their two most recent performance appraisals so that you can align the training design and delivery to that group's needs. If your learners are unemployed, try to access the standard career progression pathways for the main careers within your group so that you can contextualise the

training to that job role.

This will help you plan your training to have the greatest possible impact on participants' attitudes, behaviours, skills and knowledge. It will allow you to contextualise the resources, delivery methods, language and learning environment for optimum relevance to their lifelong pathway.

You can engage training and development participants who are resistant to change by:

- Giving them awareness
- Giving them time to prepare and plan
- Reinforcing relevance
- Defining the purpose of the training
- Illustrating soft and hard values
- Asking them for their input
- Getting to know them

RE-ENGAGE EFFICACY OF DISENGAGED LEARNERS

In my 11+ years in the education industry, I have worked in numerous educational settings, but none more challenging (albeit the most rewarding) than in the welfare to work sector where learners were forced into my training programs as a result of long-term unemployment and welfare dependency. It can be tough enough keeping the most motivated, self-enrolled learners engaged and efficacious, but people who already hate you, your program and education in general before they have even started your training course can be the ultimate challenge for your training skills.

We don't have to be in a teaching environment as extreme as this to find ourselves dealing with the challenge of re-engaging learners who have already lost their educational efficacy.

From my own experience in the education sector, here is my five-step process that will help you as an educator re-engage the disengaged.

Step 1: Remember the Purpose

Remember what you want the result or overall experience to be for you, the educational provider and the learner. This may require you to think past the immediate outcomes of the learning program.

Step 2: Create Connections

Find something in common with your learners. Find common ground, a common interest or anything that brings down the barrier of difference that may exist for the learner. As soon as we feel like we are similar to someone else, even in the remotest way, it is easier for us to listen to them, take in their suggestions and follow their advice. This doesn't necessarily mean becoming friends with your learners. It means opening up the pathways to communication.

Once you have connected with your learner, you will be in a position to connect them to the purpose of the program, the results it will bring them and the outcomes it can provide. Once they see the purpose of your course and how it applies to them, then they will be more likely to allow you to connect them to the learning program itself.

Step 3: Intercept the Negative Pattern

Remember that there is usually a difference between what people *think* they are capable of and what they are *actually* capable of. This is the stage where you change their mindset from what is likely to be a low-educational efficacy to a higher one. We need to consciously intercept the negative cycle they are in, offer another perspective, encourage, and challenge them to instigate change.

Step 4: Reinforce Their Strengths and Abilities

Often low-educational efficacy comes from a belief that they are not capable. Simply highlighting their previous successes, existing skills, qualities and strengths can be enough to start turning their motivation and engagement around.

Remind them again of the importance of the positive results, sought-after emotional, physical and experiential states and the skills they already possess. Remind them that they can get there.

Step 5: Transfer

Show them how progress has been made and how it can apply to other areas of their life. Allow progressive development by building upon the success with a slightly bigger goal, one big enough to challenge them, but not so hard that failure is inevitable. There is nothing like growing efficacy by succeeding at something that was initially perceived as a challenging task.

ACTIVITY: Engaging the Disengaged

- How will you identify and monitor the engagement and motivation levels of your learners?

- What strategies can you embed into your training programs, or add to your resources, should you face a disengaged learner?

- How can you further increase your learner motivations to succeed in your course(s) today?

> *Highlighting previous successes and existing skills can increase learner motivation and educational efficacy*

#edupreneur @CordinerSarah

THE PRINCIPLE OF LEARNING BY DOING

Adults learn through direct experience; therefore, their training and learning interventions must include active and practical participation.

There is no learning quite like getting your hands stuck in and just having a go. Allowing our learners to 'have a go' in a situation as close to real-life as possible will enhance the learning experience considerably, as we retain more information when we have to do it, instead of just see or hear about it.

As an example, on-the-job training is often the only way to learn some roles, as trying to explain, simulate or predict some situations is simply ineffective, if not impossible. Strong supporters of the learn-by-doing principle would argue that true skill, mastery and autonomy can only come from real-world practice.

This is the learn-by-doing principle of adult learning, and we can bring this element into what we are teaching regardless if we teach online or offline, or our topic's industry.

When it comes to traditional face-to-face training, this principle is easy to grasp and execute. But what about when we are delivering our training as an online course? How can you ensure that you are meeting the learn-by-doing principle of adult learning in an environment where we are not physically present to run practical exercises in person?

Are you going to be teaching a new skill to your learners in your online course? Online teaching requires very different approaches to teaching face-to-face for obvious reasons. But from my experience working with online instructors, it is not so obvious HOW to do it differently.

There are many ways to skin a cat, and there are many ways to teach people new skills. In this chapter, I will share with you three of the many effective ways of delivering excellent online training so that your courses really help your learners.

Get as visual as possible

When it comes to practical training, or teaching learners new skills, the more visual and 'live demo' you can make your course, the better.

> *When it comes to teaching learners a new skill, the more visual you can make your course the better.*

#edupreneur @CordinerSarah

Get on Camera

One way to do this is to physically get yourself on camera. Scary, I know!

But people like people, and it can significantly enhance the engagement, retention and completion rates of your course if your learners can see who is talking to them. We call this the 'talking head' video in the industry.

Your course doesn't have to be all talking head if you go for this method. Simply start with having your welcome video and the introduction of each module video feature you.

Your talking head could be as 'pro' as filming in front of a green screen. Or it could be a webcam recording, or even using your mobile phone. You don't need a Hollywood blockbuster to create an effective course. You just need to ask yourself "Is this the most visual and engaging way to teach?"

I would certainly rather see you demo how to make a cup of tea via a video you recorded on your mobile phone as you were bashing around your kitchen, than read a PDF guide on how to make the cup of tea. If you'd like to find out more about how to create talking head videos you might like to check out my online course on www.sarahcordiner.com/CreateCourse.

Screencast

Screencasting is when you use a piece of software to film or record your own computer screen live, with the sound of your voice narrating over the top.

Screencasts are great if you're showing people how to fill in a form, build a website, or anything else that could be demonstrated on a computer screen. Screencasting also allows you to speak over your PowerPoint slides with or without your webcam recording you at the same time.

There are different kinds of software that you can download for this. I personally use Camstasia Studio, which you can get a 30-day free trial to test out. If you're worried about technology, don't be. Even I figured out how to press the big red 'Record Screen' button! Camtasia has a suite of free training when you purchase the product, and YouTube is full of demo videos.

The 'DEDICT' Method of Teaching

When teaching learners a new skill, either in person or online, the DEDICT Method is a great step–by–step principle to follow to make your course engaging and impactful. Anyone learning a new skill hugely benefits from this method of teaching. The closer you can get to doing this on camera or Screencast, the better and more engaging your course will be.

Here's what to do:

D: DEMONSTRATE the task at normal speed. This helps the learners get a clear idea of what it is they are trying to achieve, the end result, the outcome, and ultimately what they are going to learn how to do.

E: EXPLAIN what you did step-by-step. Now they have seen the skills performed in real time, break it down into steps, explaining everything you do at each step.

D: DEMONSTRATE again, but this time slowly. With less in–depth explanation than the last step, now repeat the skill slowly.

I: IMITATE. Get the viewers to have a go. Encourage them to follow along, do an activity, and share their results.

C: COACH. Give feedback, further advice, scenarios where this would apply, or different scenarios where there may be an alternative way of executing the skill.

T: TEST them. Give them a practical challenge, quiz, assessment or activity.

Implementing these practical teaching principles and methods into your online courses is guaranteed to enhance the learning experience as it brings in that learn–by–doing principle of adult learning that is so critical to an effective adult learning program.

> *How to teach a skill: demonstrate at normal speed, explain, demonstrate slowly, imitate, coach, test.*

#edupreneur @CordinerSarah

THE LEARNING PRINCIPLE OF CONTEXT

Psychologist Lev Vygotsky (1934) was an avid supporter of the concept that learning is largely influenced by the learners' social and cultural situation. This was backed by Jarvis, who said that all adult learning, even self-directed learning, rarely occurs *"in splendid isolation from the world in which the learner lives; it is intimately related to that world and affected by it"*. (Jarvis, 1987. P. 87-91).

Adult learning does not occur in a vacuum. What we need or want to learn, the opportunities that are available and the manner in which we learn, are all largely determined by the society in which we live. This could be as micro as those in the shared classroom with us, to as macro as our feeling of position in the human race itself.

In regards to the wider environment, according to the likes of Belanger (1996), Glastra et a1. (2004) and Brysk (2003), the nature of adult learning is shaped by three main characteristics:

1. Demographics
2. Globalisation
3. Technology

When you are designing and delivering your own training programs, ensure that you have considered if any of these factors could impact the environment, and subsequently, the learning experience.

Globalisation

As a simple example, I teach online course creation and, 119lobalization has had an impact on my course. Because we now have a global marketplace, we accept payments for our courses in many different currencies and therefore have different payment processors and tax systems to think about, and that is something that then has to be covered. If I didn't teach in a global environment, this wouldn't be a consideration at all.

Technology

A few years ago, the content of my online course would have been completely different to what it is today. As technology changes, my lectures and content change, as well, so that they match the ever-changing technological environment that we live in.

Demographics

If I was enrolled in a training course where I was significantly younger or older than the rest of my colleagues, my learning experience would be influenced by that demographical environment, and again that would mean that we would have to plan and deliver our training accordingly if we wanted to create the optimum learning experience for *everyone*.

Context

Further, a number of contextual factors can influence an adult learner's experience, some of which are illustrated by *Maslow's Hierarchy of Need*s shown below. The first four layers of the pyramid are what Maslow calls 'deficiency needs'.

An individual does not necessarily feel anything if they are met, but feels anxious or unfulfilled if they are *not* met. The deficiency needs are physiological, while the top level is concerned with growth and psychological needs. The higher needs in this hierarchy only come into focus when the lower needs in the pyramid are satisfied.

Maslow's Hierarchy of Needs:

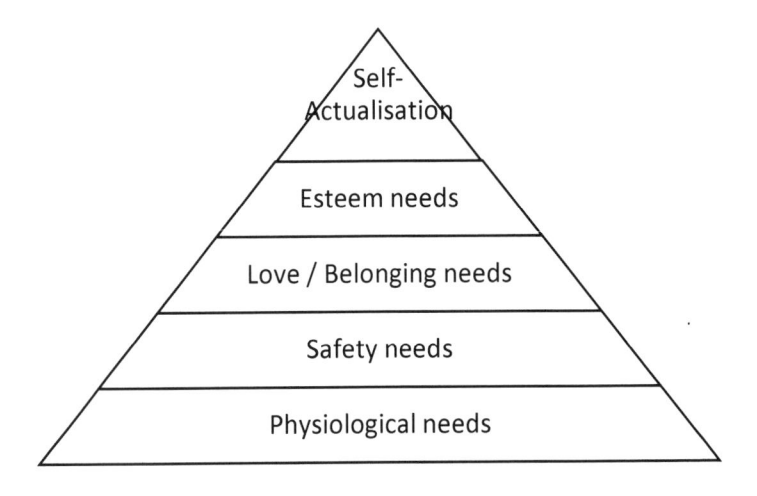

- Self-Actualisation
- Esteem needs
- Love / Belonging needs
- Safety needs
- Physiological needs

In a classroom situation, this would require the facilitator to control conditions in a way that would satisfy the lower levels of the model in order to allow for the top parts (learning and growth) to actually take place, aside from being nourished, warm and safe.

"Such conditions are freedom to speak, freedom to do what

one wishes so long as no harm is done to others, freedom to express one's self freedom to investigate and seek for information, freedom to defend one's self justice, fairness, honesty, orderliness in the group are examples of such preconditions for basic need satisfactions." (Maslow, 1943. P.19-25).

Essentially, Maslow suggests that personal growth and development is much more accessible when the fundamental survival needs of your learners have been satisfied. However, this theory has its doubters, as such concepts could be arguably different in many learning environments.

Take prisons, for example. In regards to the particular prisons I have worked in, despite my learners being physically behind bars, the learners' survival needs (e.g. food, shelter and warmth) are being met. In class, there was an agreed understanding that everyone was free to express their opinions without fear of ridicule or judgment, thus allowing a safe learning environment.

Despite many of them being in an unpredictable, unsafe and 'unloved' environment, they still managed to achieve academically in the prison education system.

The research that I conducted into art education in correctional settings supports part of Maslow's theory. My findings illustrated the importance of a conditioned learning environment to the learners. There were many references to the teacher, the feelings they get when in the class and how the atmosphere impacts on their overall experiences.

Questionnaire feedback from incarcerated learners in my study indicated answers such as:

"*It's always cold in the classroom.*"

"*It would be better if we could open the windows for air. It's too stuffy.*"

It is difficult to imagine how these learners could have had any productive learning experiences at all when such basic needs are not being met, if you are looking at it from Maslow's perspective. In fact, there are many examples of learner achievement in educational attainment despite terrible physical conditions. Obviously, creating the optimum learning environment is always going to enhance the learning experience for the better.

Finally, other ways that context can influence adult learning is to consider the situation the adult is learning in, such as whether they are learning in a formal or informal manner. For example, if they are in an institution, a community centre, taking an exam or researching at home on the internet can affect the emotions someone has whilst they are learning, the kind of experience they have and, ultimately, how much they learn from it. It is also wise to consider the different relationships of power and the social place of the learner in a learning situation.

As a further example, learners who have enrolled *themselves* in a self-study personal development course are likely to feel some degree of choice, control and influence over their own learning. Whereas in a learning environment such as a prison, there are a few more restrictions, and although the learners are responsible for their own work, they certainly don't consider themselves to have a significant degree of power over what they are learning.

ACTIVITY: Planning Your Learning Environment

When it comes to considering the things that are going to affect the training and delivery of our programs, it's absolutely critical to plan the environment in which it's going to be learned.

1. How does your learning environment enhance or restrict the learning process?
2. In what ways could you further improve upon the learning environment?
3. Where will your learning most likely take place?
4. Will the environment be the same for all learners?
5. Is it an authentic or simulated workplace?
6. Is it in a college, school, community building or their own home?
7. Will it be wholly or partly online, distance or remote?
8. Will any of it be in a geographically remote location or involve travel?
9. What are the health and safety considerations that need to be made in the environment?
10. Will there be refreshments, air conditioning, appropriate lighting, seating, a comfortable room temperature and seating?

THE LEARNING PRINCIPLE OF RELEVANCE AND READINESS

Have you ever had to sit through a meeting where everything being discussed has nothing to do with your role or even your department? For those who have, you'd know that trying to maintain concentration is difficult, even for the most motivated of people. This is because when we feel that information is not relevant to us, our brain turns off and 'saves it's batteries' for something else. If your learners do not feel like your training is relevant to them, their willingness, or readiness to learn, will be unsubstantial at best.

This characteristic of adult learning considers an adult's readiness to learn, or the need for relevance in their educational programs. This refers to their willingness and preparation to get started on their learning journey

It proposes that the content of a training program must be meaningful and relevant to the adult learners, their lives and their business. They have to clearly see why and how this is important to them personally and how it applies to their life.

The immediate value of the learning needs to be clearly understood by the learner. If they can't see how they personally can apply the learning to their own life and roles, motivation towards the training intervention will be significantly reduced.

Knowles suggests that as a person matures, his readiness to learn becomes increasingly relevant and focussed to the developmental tasks of his social role and to help him effectively cope with life situations that such roles entail.

In short, the theory of this relevancy concept is that adults must see a reason for learning something in order to hit the gas pedal, enroll and fully engage and benefit from the experience.

There are a few ways that you can design and deliver your training programs to ensure that you meet this principle in your courses. Adults are ready to learn when they see your course as something that they want to learn or master.

Second to wanting to learn the skills is feeling that they need to learn whatever your course is teaching in order to get better at their job or life in some way. An adult's readiness to learn will increase when they can see that taking on the new information, skill, knowledge or competency will help them directly improve their own world.

Set clear goals and outcomes

Adult learners focus on the goals and outcomes that the learning will provide them, and they then use these to decide if those outcomes are *relevant* to them and if they are *ready* to acquire those outcomes.

Ensure that your course sales pages and descriptions clearly explain the outcomes they will get in as much detail as possible, in language that is most likely to be used by your target learner so that the highest opportunity exists for them to see the relevancy of your training.

Break your outcomes down into their smallest parts. For

example, if you were teaching a course on how to make a sandwich, don't just say in the description "*In this course you will learn how to make the world's most delicious sandwich.*"

Break down everything they will learn about making that sandwich, listing specific learning outcomes that cover every stage of the process, e.g., you may create learning outcomes for each of these stages:

- shopping and selecting the ingredients
- how to tell if the ingredients are fresh and ripe
- different types of bread and how they affect the taste of the sandwich
- how to safely and effectively slice the bread
- the correct layering of the sandwich filling
- the perfect amount of butter and how to spread it without breaking the bread
- how to cut the sandwich into the most aesthetically pleasing shape

Of course, this is a silly sandwich example, but by the time you have done the equivalent in your own topic, you will find that you have covered significantly more outcomes than your course originally would have described and have subsequently multiplied the opportunity for learners to see your course's value and relevance to them.

In summary, adult learners:

- want timely learning, i.e. they only want to learn things that are relevant and applicable right now
- seek meaningful learning experiences
- need clear learning objectives so that they can

decide if the learning is directly relevant to their immediate wants and needs.
- realise that learning is applicable to their work or other responsibilities and is of value to them.

Therefore, course creators must identify objectives and explicit learning outcomes for adult participants before the course begins. It also means that theories and concepts must be related to a setting familiar to the participants. This is called contextualisation.

THE LEARNING PRINCIPLE OF CONTEXTUALISATION

Another way to enhance learner engagement and retention in your training, as well as meet the relevancy principle of adult learning, is to contextualise.

Contextualisation is a practice you will need to become very familiar with if you're working in the training design and development space, or the training and delivery space as a trainer. This means making sure that we are adapting, or customising, training in a way that makes it 'tailored' for use in a specific environment.

> *Contextualisation is an extremely powerful teaching and learning technique. Use it to make each learner feel like your training was made especially for them.*

#edupreneur @CordinerSarah

I remember being in a leadership seminar once where the instructor spent the entire morning dropping golf metaphors as he taught us about leadership. As he referred to a bad leadership example, he backed it up with a joke about a bad golf swing. As he provided a strategy for successful leadership, he slipped in a reference to getting a hole in one.

This is a fantastic example of contextualising IF we had been golfers! If this seminar had been about leadership in the golfing industry, then this instructor would have absolutely nailed the contextualisation of this talk. Using familiar concepts and references that they are passionate about means that the new learning would be more rapidly constructed into understanding than it would without the golf references.

However, the fact that not a single one of us in the room was a golfer meant that half the room was asleep (switching off because it didn't feel relevant) and the other half had no idea what he was talking about.

Contextualisation is an extremely powerful teaching and learning technique when the *right* circumstantial and environmental references are used.

The word 'context' means "*the circumstances that form the setting for an event, statement, or idea, and in terms of which it can be fully understood*". When it comes to training, this means how we design and deliver our training to the circumstances or environment in which our learners live in or will apply it.

For example, if I was teaching a course called How To Create Online Courses to the staff at a training institution such as a college, I would deliver it differently, use different language and give them different activities to practice their skills than if I was teaching the exact same course to solopreneur business owners even though the outcomes are the same.

Why? Because they are applying their own learning in different environments (contexts), and the most effective training and trainers adapt and modify their programs for each group's unique context.

Contextualise to increase your content output

Sometimes, when we have very narrow topics or highly niched fields of practice, it can be hard to find new content to teach or use as content marketing. I have found that we can use the concept of contextualisation to significantly broaden our topic and appeal to more learners, without deviating from our specialisation.

Here is a way that I have contextualised a range of seemingly irrelevant topics with my concept of 'Edupreneurship' and course creation to make my topic appealing to those who may not have seen it as relevant.

1. First, I listed everything that my target audience (Edupreneurs and course creators) do, use or need to do to be successful.
2. Then I added the words 'For Edupreneurs' at the end.
3. Then I came up with blog posts and lectures in the topics I could cover
4. Then I approached other subject matter experts and did a joint work with them (eg webinars and interviews) on the topics I am not an expert in, and I directed the entire conversation to *my* audience (in these cases, edupreneurs).
5. Then I used the expert webinars as an information source for more blogs and tutorial videos for my training. My audience got expert advice, tailored to application in their context, and the expert got exposure to my audience.

Here is one of my lists of training topics that are not directly about training and course creation, that I have 'contextualised' to make *relevant* to my learners:

- Google apps for Edupreneurs
- Facebook for Edupreneurs
- YouTube for Edupreneurs
- Twitter for Edupreneurs
- Wordpress for Edupreneurs
- Blogging for Edupreneurs
- Creating books and ebooks for Edupreneurs
- Linkedin for Edupreneurs
- Snapchat for Edupreneurs
- Public speaking skills for Edupreneurs
- Launch strategies for Edupreneurs
- LeadPages for Edupreneurs
- PR and Media for Edupreneurs
- Entrepreneurship for Edupreneurs
- Webinars for Edupreneurs
- Lead magnet creation for Edupreneurs
- Email marketing for Edupreneurs
- Podcasting for Edupreneurs
- Graphic design for Edupreneurs
- Partnerships and referral marketing for Edupreneurs
- Building an email list for Edupreneurs
- SEO for Edupreneurs

As well as making your training more relevant and engaging for your learners, contextualisation can help address:

- different learner profiles
- specific equipment and tools

- specific policies, procedures and processes
- the physical environment they learn or work in
- legislative requirements in that context

By changing activities, terminology, case scenarios, metaphors and supporting documentation, we can provide highly relevant training in any circumstance.

As another example, if I was writing a management course, I could have a generic course that covered management skills in general, a global topic that has similar concepts regardless of the industry the manager is in. However, if I was delivering that course to a group of education managers, I'd contextualise and adapt my training to bring in the unique managerial experiences and considerations in an educational context.

I would give examples of classroom management, managing teachers, managing students, managing school rules, managing school conditions, reference educational legislation that had to be adhered to, use education industry terminology, use policies from the specific learning institution as references and guidelines, and so on.

Contextualisation is NOT about altering the learning outcomes or objectives. It's about modifying the *WAY* you transmit the training so that it applies and has relevance to the learner's world as they know it.

If we were teaching a course on work health and safety, we could encourage learners to gather safe working procedures and company policies from *their own* businesses or workplaces to make the generic topic directly apply to their own environment

Contextualising means adapting as far as we possibly can the content, the delivery, the language, the methods of assessment and the examples used, so that it is aligned to those particular learners, in that particular environment.

Contextualising means adapting our course content so that it is as aligned as possible to each individual learner's circumstances. #edupreneur @CordinerSarah

There are Limits to Contextualisation

When I say "adapt as far as we possibly can," it is because we have to proceed with a degree of caution when contextualising. What we can't do is contextualise training so much that it alters the learning outcomes, and subsequently becomes a different course.

Remember my experience at the leadership seminar? I would have argued that it was more of a theoretical training session on golf, rather than leadership. If we over-contextualise we miss the whole point of what we were trying to teach in the first place.

We cannot change the conditions of assessment, or what the student will be able to do, know and feel by the end of the course because that would mean it is a different course that produces a different result. We simply want to contextualise the *way* that it's delivered and some of the delivery materials used, to enhance understanding, learning, the application of that learning, the theory and the practice in a particular place.

Capitalise on their interests

Another way to embed the principle of relevance and context into your online courses is to allow participants to choose projects that reflect their own interests within a specific subject area.

We succeed and excel when we are doing what we love. They will love their training if it involves their passion. The more you can find ways to bring in the element of joy, hobbies and interests to learner activities, exercises and projects, the more engaged and successful they will be.

Knowles states that "*adults are practical.*" Therefore, by focusing on the aspects of a lesson most useful to them in their work and their roles, they will be more likely to learn.

Many adults learn purely for the joy of learning as well as being in pursuit of a certain result. By adding some emotive references to their passions, their readiness to learn will increase as they will see the relevance and purpose of it to them and what they love.

> *Give them love AND reason. Many adults learn purely for the joy of learning as well as being in pursuit of a certain result.*

#edupreneur @CordinerSarah

Sarah Cordiner

THE LEARNING PRINCIPLE OF EXPERIENCE

Learning something valuable is not restricted to the classroom.

> *"All learning is based on experience."*
> *(Moon, 2004, p.119).*

Adult learners need to be able to *draw upon* their experiences, as well as be given the chance to gain experience, to have truly successful and transformational training experiences.

Experiential learning for GAINING experience

One part of the experience principle of adult learning refers to designing and delivering training that has the learners' experiences in mind. However, in this first section, we will talk about the importance of designing and delivering training that *provides* small educational experiences and outcomes via that real-time act of doing.

Training needs to be contextualised to use language with which they are familiar. We need to select case scenarios and examples that they can relate to, as well as refer to their direct past life, work and social experiences to bring the meaning of the learning into their world, as they understand it.

As a person matures, they accumulate a history and foundation of life experiences and knowledge, both good and bad. These could include work-related activities, family responsibilities and previous education, that all add to an increasing resource for learning.

This is a very important concept in adult education, due to the influence that past experiences can have on our learners perceptions of education and their academic abilities. But it can also be influenced by the existence of preconceived notions which generate certain expectations from education and its processes, which again can be good or bad depending on the experience.

The fact that children have little previous experience to influence their thoughts, feelings and reactions to new information is reflected by the more didactic teaching methods they experience in the classroom.

Drawing upon my own experiences as an adult educator, particularly in prison and welfare to work environments, or with groups of low educational attainment, I have observed a disconnect, particularly with unskilled adults who see learning as something inseparable from formal school and training courses.

Their experiences of formal learning are often painful memories of humiliation, boredom and failure. Based on such experiences, they have decided that learning is not for them. However, the right approach to training, which draws upon the experiences of learners, allows them to recognise that throughout the course of their lives they have learnt many things such as a verbal language, to drive, to raise children, to cook, to operate equipment, and so on.

Many adults I have worked with in these circumstances like

to learn by doing, by direct experience. They like to learn about things of personal interest or obvious relevance to their lives.

For example, one of my prison students was a tattooist before his incarceration, and he spent much of his time in the art classes deeply consumed in designing new tattoos, which with my guidance was done in a way that met assessment criteria.

His evaluation of the course was very positive indeed. He was so delighted with his evidence-based success (the attainment of a certificate) that he found the confidence to enroll in other education courses offered by the prison, and he approached them with a positive and motivated attitude. The discovery of his own ability to succeed in something 'educational' transformed not only his whole perspective on education, but also the way he viewed himself and his abilities in relation to education.

Kegan (2000) and Taylor (2005) call this effect of an experience 'transformational or transformative learning,' and my example illustrates its power in adult learning. In my model of the development of educational efficacy, I call it 'efficacious education'. Transformative learning refers to a dramatic or fundamental change in the way we see ourselves and the way in which we live. It is 'changing what we know,' according to Kegan, 2000. p3).

Another aspect of this concept would perhaps include that of experiential education. Kolb describes experience as "*the source of learning and development*" (Kolb, 1984).

This idea has had a dramatic impact on the design and development of lifelong learning models, which can be traced back to 450 BC when dictum Confucius wrote, "*Tell me, and I will forget. Show me, and I may remember. Involve me, and I will understand*" (Confucius, 450BC).

Ensure that the design of your learning programs allow for the previous experiences of your learners, and the actual process of learning and teaching itself creates new experiences for your learners in relation to a personal interest and life-relevant area.

ACTIVITY: Bringing in the Experience

- How do your current training programs allow for the integration and consideration of adult learners' experiences?

- How can you improve the planning, delivery and resources you use to better incorporate a learner's experience?

- What can you do to gather information about your learner's past experiences before they start your course?

THE LEARNING PRINCIPLE OF REFLECTION

In mid-2015, I felt like I didn't have an ounce of breath left in me.

The business I'd worked so hard to build took a brutal hit when a number of my clients were unexpectedly affected by a sudden Federal budget cut, and it left them unable to see their contracts through with my company MainTraining (www.maintraining.com.au).

I lost all twenty-three of my team members. I had to shut down the office and sell everything in it, which didn't even touch paying off the high six-figure debt I had to pay in staff wages, leases and tax bills.

I was facing liquidation. And I had just found out I was pregnant.

As the Western Australian resources bust and budget cuts began claiming businesses like mine all around me, I knew I had two very distinct choices:

a) Take the much easier route and fold. Follow the advice of everyone around me, which was "*Know when to let go, Sarah. You tried, and it didn't work. Go and do something else*".

OR

b) Realise that I got myself into that situation and that I could get myself out. See this experience as a powerful lesson, one that was giving me an opportunity to adapt to a changing economy, to become a more innovative business owner and to ultimately become a better teacher.

I knew I couldn't give up.

With tears streaming down my face, the weight of the world suffocating me and a feeling of failure so cutting that my heart felt like it was bleeding, I dragged myself through each and every day knowing that I had to make a better world for the tiny life inside me and everyone else who might learn from my lesson, too.

Everyone kept telling me to give up. To not put so much pressure on myself. To rest. To LET GO.

But they didn't understand.

I wasn't holding onto anything in the past. It was gone. I was building a new future.

Day by day, I built. I learned. I created. I dared. I pushed. I cried. I tried. I ran. I climbed. I shared. I gave.

In the following eighteen months, I built well over 100 online courses.

I enrolled over 6,000 students in 121 countries. I won multiple awards, traveled the world as a speaker, became a two-times international number 1 best-selling author, and even got my own TV show (Course Creators on www.brin.ai). I increased my original profit margin from 31% to 60%, increased business by 1,900% and now have a global client base. I was also listed by The Huffington Post as one of the *'Top 50 Must-Follow Female Entrepreneurs for 2017.'*

But my biggest success? NOT GIVING UP.

If I had given up back then when the world seemed so heavy on my shoulders, when everyone was telling me to, none of those accolades would be mine and 6,000+ people would not be educated.

Success is not found in your moments of glory. It's showing stamina, determination, commitment and unwavering dedication to your mission when things are hard.

Success is not when days are going great for you. It's continuing to get out of bed and trying to put one foot in front of the other when the days are dark and frightening.

Success is not in winning. Success is in the good that you choose to do in the face of failure.

I'm not a success story. I'm an "*eleven years of never quitting*" story. If I had quit, I would not have been given the opportunity to innovate and find new ways of doing and delivering what I loved.

As much as the experience was agonizing, and still leaves scars on my life and shadows in my memories, I can now look back with gratitude at what a blessing and invaluable learning experience it was to me as a business owner, a leader and a woman.

As I was reflecting on all of this while driving through my local suburb, the song '*The Greatest*' by S.I.A was playing on the radio in the background. As I listened to the lyrics, a tear randomly sneaked out of my eye.

As it trickled down my cheek, I realised just what a wonderful gift of education and experience that my beautiful failures have been. I wouldn't be anything without them. I'd be less still, if I'd given up in the face of them.

My tears turned into a smile as two years of pain, anger and bitterness suddenly washed away and the true lesson of it all actualised before me.

THIS is the power of reflection. Using it in your training programs can facilitate dramatic shifts in personal development, perspectives, skill and lifelong learning.

At the time, it was sheer hell. I was filled with bitterness and rage. My staff didn't take it very well, and I didn't deal with them not dealing with it well, either. In fact, the redundancy and shut down phase was a disaster, and at the time all I could do was feel sorry for myself and grow an ever-increasing hatred towards my previously much loved team. Everything just felt so unfair.

Despite powering on and dragging myself forward day by day and seeming fairly proactive on the surface for doing so, I was emotionally and mentally stuck in the reactive. I blamed the Prime Minister for slashing my clients' budgets. I blamed my clients for not being able to give us a dissolution period. I blamed my staff for wanting their redundancy and superannuation money. I blamed my previous contracts for being finished so they weren't there to save me. I blamed myself for being a dreadful business woman and dropping all the balls. I was super angry and felt as if the world was being frightfully cruel to me.

But time started to pass. The rage subsided into disappointment, and disappointment fizzled into "*Well, that was a rough ride.*" That eventually dissolved into "*Wow, thank goodness that happened because look how much I learned.*"

> *#Success isn't based on what goes right. It's about showing resilience when things go wrong. Have strategies for keeping your learners resilient.*
> #edupreneur @CordinerSarah

Although off-topic slightly, I want to share my reflections on this because it's not only been key to my phoenix-like turn around, but it also drives home the importance and power of reflection in adult learning.

I would not have had the chance to learn any of these things, my business and brand would not be where it is, 6,000 people would not be educated, my many accolades would not exist, my global following would have disappeared, and I would not be the leader that I am today had all of this *not* happened.

- What if I had never reflected upon any of these things?
- What if I'd just sat back and continued to feel sorry for myself?
- What if instead of looking at the future, I had only looked upon the past and what had gone wrong instead of what had been gained?

I am sure the depression and severe anxiety that temporarily consumed me at the time would have eaten me entirely.

I am sure that my business would have been well and truly liquidated and that I probably would have lost my house and assets paying off the debt I was left with.

I am sure that I would be harbouring much anger, hatred and hurt.

REFLECTION enabled me to completely reverse this experience, from a bad one to one that I now see as truly the best thing that ever happened to me.

It is reflection that has made me strong, happy, and powerful, and has ultimately been responsible for me going on to change the world—not just my own circumstances—for the better.

As you can see, reflection and reflective practices are seriously powerful tools in our educational armoury. They help our students learn about themselves, their world and their capabilities at a whole other level.

My story proves that lives can be fundamentally changed using reflection as a learning tool, and in the rest of this chapter I am going to share some tips for how you can include this amazing adult learning practice to enhance the learning experience and outcomes in your training programs.

Experience alone may not constitute new learning that can be applied in other situations. Not considering what was wrong, right, good, bad, significant or insignificant in an event, to ignore or forget it after it has happened, leaves little to no room for any kind of learning to accumulate from it. In order for one to learn from an experience, one must reflect upon it.

> *In order to truly learn from an experience, you have to reflect on it first.*
> @CordinerSarah #edupreneur

Reflection facilitates deep and complex learning to uncover the *meaning* behind an experience. Reflection causes a process of learning known as scaffolding, which draws upon past experiences, our cognitive, behavioural, emotional and physical recollections to construct and synthesize new meanings. This then allows us to apply new knowledge to circumstances outside of the context in which it was learned. Essentially, reflection is the synthesisation of meaningful transferable skills

In the book *Learning and Leading with Habits of Mind*, Costa and Kallick state "*if we want them [learners] to use habits of mind such as applying past knowledge to new situations, thinking about thinking (metacognition), and remaining open to continuous learning—we must teach them strategies to derive rich meaning from their experiences.*"

We need to find ways to get our learners to continuously reflect and self-assess if their approaches, methods, actions, progress and development have been sufficient and of value, and how they can apply their new skills and knowledge to other contexts.

The reflection process, such as keeping a diary of significant events and revisiting them later on from various perspectives, can show learners that they actually learnt a considerable amount more than they initially thought. If only 5% of learning is retained in most formal, didactic forms of teaching, reflection is a great way to revisit, revise and re-engage with content that otherwise may have been forgotten.

Having been a reflective trainer and learner all of my professional life, I still find the reflection process very revealing with respect to my progress and development. It never fails to empower me and fill me with a real sense of ability and achievement. The process itself allows learners to realise and better understand themselves and others, such as behaviour, motives for it and the cause and effects of their interactions with others. This learning may not have occurred had I not had the opportunity to reflect, and so it is with many adult learners.

Despite its benefits however, we again must ensure that we do not use this one method of adult learning in isolation. Having only our own experiences to reflect upon, and our own opinions to reflect upon them with, we are significantly missing the learning available from considering the viewpoints and opinions of others, as well as the importance of theoretical learning in conjunction with our reflections of an experience.

In addition, there may be times when experiential or

reflective learning is not appropriate, such as when substantial amounts of new information are required. Examples of this would be revising facts for a necessary exam or a doctor learning which illness each medication treats.

Here are 6 strategies that you could use to facilitate reflective learning:

1. Get learners to deconstruct their thinking by journaling and regularly reviewing the journal entries.

2. Discussion. This could be in groups, in pairs, with the facilitator, with themselves or with an imaginary person or group.

3. They could create a presentation about their problem-solving processes—what they did, what thought processes and emotional experiences they went through, what trials and errors they encountered and what knowledge, skills, strengths and experiences they used to overcome them or change strategies, and what they will do if they face a similar task in the future.

4. Get learners to act like journalists and interview one another about the learning. It could be at the end of a major project or at the end of a short session. The process of writing explorative and thought-provoking questions sparks their own metacognitive and reflective thought processes. By conducting an interview as interviewee and interviewer, they also develop other essential transferable skills in the reflective process, such

as communication, inquisition, questioning, listening, empathy and learning from the processes used by others.

5. Develop well-thought out questions for your learners to answer.

    a. Such questions could include:
    b. In reflection of the past [*duration*], in what ways has your thinking about [*topic*] changed?
    c. What thinking processes or patterns (metacognition) have you used to better understand [*topic*]?
    d. In what ways will your new understandings and ways of thinking inform the next stage of your actions in [*topic*]?
    e. What further insights have these new ways of thinking informed your practice/work/life?

6. Get your learners to regularly revisit an individual development plan or action plan, which includes review dates and reflective questions on progress made and the impact the development has had beyond their skills acquisition.

"Reflection in education allows learners to better understand themselves and others" #edupreneur @CordinerSarah

ACTIVITY: Encourage Reflective Learning

1. What methods of reflection do you currently use in your practice?

   _____

   _____

2. How can you further contribute to your learning processes using reflective learning strategies?

   _____

   _____

Sarah Cordiner

THE LEARNING PRINCIPLE OF THE SENSES

Adult learners need multi-sensory learning and teaching methodologies. We must ensure that our learning interventions have appropriately proportioned delivery techniques that meet the needs of audio, visual, reading/writing, kinaesthetic, dependent and independent learning preferences.

The Dunn and Dunn Learning Style Model is a great reference for getting a bigger picture of all of the variables that have been found to affect a learner's educational achievements.

Here is an overview to help you plan and prepare for effective training programs.

Stimuli	Considerations
Environmental elements	Where do they prefer to learn? • Sound • Light • Temperature
Emotional elements	How much intervention will they need to stay on task? How structured do they need the program to be? • Motivation • Conformity

	- Responsibility - Task persistence - Structure
Sociological elements	How much interaction with others do they prefer to have? How much involvement do they want from the trainer? - Alone - Pairs - Group work - Teacher-led - Variety
Physiological elements	When and how do they prefer to learn? - Auditory - Visual - Kinaesthetic - Food & water intake - Time of day - Mobility
Psychological elements	How do they process information and absorb new ideas? - Analytical - Global - Impulsive - Reflective

GET IN THE 'MODE'

In this chapter, we will look at what that means for you in terms of how it affects the building of your learning product or program.

As we have seen above, according to the Dunn and Dunn model of learning styles, students learning can be affected by the following:

- The learning environment (sound, light, temperature, seating design)
- Their emotional state at the time of learning (motivation, task persistence, responsibility/conformity, structure)
- Their social learning preferences (learning alone, in pairs, in a small group of peers, as part of a team, with an adult, with a mixture of all of these)
- Physiological factors (perceptual strengths, time of day, need for food intake, mobility while learning)
- Psychological processing preferences (global/analytic, impulsive/reflective).

To create effective adult learning programs, carefully consider each of the factors above with your specific target group and individual learner needs in mind, and design your program, content and delivery to nurture the most optimum learning experience.

One of the first things we need to consider is whether we have designed our program for the four main types of learners:

- visual learners
- audio learners
- kinaesthetic learners
- Reading and writing learners

The Visual Learner:

Our visual learners like to see. They are people that learn best by watching, seeing images and observing. To ensure that your training is engaging for the visual learner, make sure that your courses contain elements such as the following:

- Videos
- Animations
- PowerPoint slides
- Pictures/images
- Drawings/doodles
- Diagrams
- Mindmaps
- Visualisations
- Flashcards
- Opportunities to write, highlight and colour
- Maps
- Physical demonstrations that they can watch

You can now get highly professional and very affordable animated videos and PowerPoint slides using web sites such as fiverr.com and upwork.com.

I like to further enhance the visual learning component of

my tutorial videos by having myself on screen in front of my PowerPoint slides, which is called a 'talking head' video. This is not because I have some egotistical desire to be on everyone's computer screens. It actually comes from the simple fact that people relate to and engage with a human more than to a slide show.

The type of training I teach is very theoretical and classroom-based and therefore would be very dull and have a real of lack of interaction if my human face wasn't there to engage them. This simple combination of my face and the PowerPoint slides behind me ensures that I am maximizing the learning opportunity and learning potential of this program because it meets the visual learners needs considerably. It also meets some other modes of learning too.

How can you make your training more visual for your learners?

> *All learners are different. Ensure you have designed your training to cater for different needs, styles and preferences.*

#edupreneur @CordinerSarah

The Auditory Learner:

Another mode of learning is auditory learning. Auditory learners simply learn better by listening. This doesn't mean that they don't learn in any of the other modes. It just means that hearing new information is their strongest and most natural form of acquiring it.

Quite simply, anything that allows your learners to hear new information will help the auditory learner. Below are some suggestions for various components you can include in your training courses to ensure that your training is engaging for the auditory learner:

1. Pay attention to the volume, pitch, tone, diction and variation of your voice
2. Ensure that they don't have to sit silently for extended periods of time
3. Create an MP3 or other audio version of your training for them to listen to
4. Don't have too much reading content in your course
5. Tell stories
6. Make things rhyme, be melodious or have memorable tunes or songs
7. Verbally explain what you are doing when you are demonstrating tasks
8. Encourage group discussions and conversations between the students
9. Provide opportunities for verbal communication such as question and answer forums, telephone calls, or live interactive webinars

Auditory learners don't just learn by listening to you speaking. They also learn by listening to themselves speak.

Therefore, including any activities in your training course that encourages the learners to do any of the following will also support the auditory learner considerably:

- Speak aloud to themselves

- Record audio of themselves
- Teach and explain things to others
- Produce and submit videos or audios as part of their assessment
- Recite or repeat the learning

This is, by no means, an exhaustive list of ways that you can enhance training for your auditory learners. However, including at least one or two elements from the list above will help you create engaging training programs for all of your auditory participants.

What can you do to make your training more engaging for auditory learners?

Are there any items that we've missed from our list?

The Theory and Principles of Creating Effective Training Courses

The Kinaesthetic Learner:

Kinaesthetic learning (also known as tactile learning) explains how learners best acquire new skills and knowledge by doing. This means making your training as practical, hands on and active as possible.

When designing and delivering effective adult learning programs, consider including as many of the following as possible:

1. The more you teach from a place of "This is HOW you do this" instead of "Let me tell you about this," the more engaged your kinaesthetic learners are going to be
2. Provide Screencast demos that allow them to follow along and copy as they watch
3. Make practical written activities by getting them to write notes on post-its and stick them on the wall
4. Encourage activities when they can be physically present with other people. Kinaesthetic learners are very tactile and even like to touch other people when they are talking to them
5. Create physical activities and practical games
6. Keep lectures short
7. Give them templates to fill in
8. Insert a practical activity or exercise every 15 minutes
9. Resist giving your students all of the answers and instead provide problem-solving activities
10. Include challenges and competitions
11. Kinaesthetic learners like to try new things, so instead of always explaining activities before they start, allow

kinesthetic learners the opportunity to jump in at the deep end and figure it out for themselves
12. Kinesthetic learners enjoy touching things so provide props in your training for learners to hold and play with
13. Make sure that they are not forced to sit and listen for extended periods of time
14. Include arts, crafts and model making, drawing materials, textured and coloured materials
15. Set up role play activities
16. Create simulations and replica environments
17. Get them to conduct experiments and investigations
18. Incorporate field trips or site visits
19. Incorporate workplace learning elements or work experience
20. Give them projects
21. Get them to collect evidence of their knowledge and competence and create a portfolio

If you would like any help or guidance on making your training more engaging for all of the different learning types, modes and preferences, do not hesitate to get in touch with me to book a consultation.

KNOW YOUR GLOBAL VS. YOUR ANALYTICAL

Global and analytical are the two major information-processing styles that learners can fall into. By understanding the difference between these two styles, we can be better prepared to create transformational adult learning programs.

Global:

As the name would suggest, global learners are people who learn better by approaching new concepts, skills and knowledge from a much bigger viewpoint. If you can give your global learners the opportunity to see their learning program, and all learning within it, from a bird's eye point of view, you will be helping them considerably. If you want to give a global learner an engaging learning experience, then give them the bigger picture.

> *If you want to give a global learner an engaging learning experience, then give them the 'bigger picture' when explaining new concepts instead of going into detail.*
> *#edupreneur @CordinerSarah*

They get very bored and frustrated with details and long winded explanations. They are the kind of learner who has already flicked through their entire workbook and figured out the general gist of the program (which is all they need), before you've even asked them to open the first page. They are also perfectly happy to jump straight to chapter 14 without even glancing at chapters 1-13, simply because that's the most relevant or interesting to them.

If you have bullet points on your slides, they will already have skipped through to reading the last one before you've even started explaining the first one. And they will immediately proceed to get bored and frustrated as they already know what you're going to say, and they don't need it repeated.

If they are taking an online course, they will scroll through all of the lecture titles and happily watch the videos in a non-sequential order based on what stands out or rings through as applicable for them. They will even happily feel like they have completed the course without having watched all of the videos.

To enable a better learning experience for the global learner, make sure that your learning programs have a very clear curriculum and overview. Make sure that the learning content is open to be engaged with at any time (global learners hate drip-fed content) and that videos have an 'increase the speed' function so that they can skip past what they don't feel is necessary.

Analytical

Analytical learners, on the other hand, like things to go in order, in a perfectly consecutive, sequential pattern. They like their learning to be presented to them in step-by-step stages, with each step logically following on from the last. Analytical learners love drip-fed content, especially if it is delivered in accordance with a stringent schedule provided to them before the start of the course.

If they feel like a step is missing or has been skipped, they can feel annoyed, frustrated, and hard-done by, as if something has been taken away from them. The analytical learner will not appreciate being asked to work on chapter 3, unless they have fully completed chapters 1 and 2 first and in that order.

> *Analytical learners like things to go perfectly in order, in a consecutive, sequential pattern. Stick to the course schedule with these types of learners.*

#edupreneur @CordinerSarah

If you wish to engage your analytical learners, make sure your courses follow a very clear structure, plan and schedule, explain all of your content in detail, and do not miss any steps or bullet points when presenting.

CAPTURE HEARTS AND MINDS

All of our training should include a personal and personable element, that is, learning content and experiences that connect to the human soul.

> *People learn better when you capture their heart AND their mind.*
> *#edupreneur @CordinerSarah*

First, this is important because people are more likely to remember and recall information when they've been anchored by some kind of emotion. Secondly, connecting the hearts of our students to what we are teaching nurtures passion for the subject matter and an association of your training to their bigger life purpose and existential meaning. Finally, some people will simply only be moved into action if they can see how there is a nurturing, loving, generous, softer meaning to what you are teaching.

As an example, if you are teaching a course on entrepreneurship and you want to engage a heart-driven learner, here is a good and bad way to entice them into your program:

Bad: *"This course on entrepreneurship will provide you with the strategies to triple your income."*

Good: *"This course on entrepreneurship will provide you with the strategies to make a positive difference to the world with your business services."*

Considering these heart-centred learners when designing and delivering your training increases engagement levels and maintains high rates of retention and completion of your courses, not to mention those 5-star reviews that touch our own hearts as trainers!

Look at movies, stories and even front-page news articles. They just wouldn't be the same if they didn't make us laugh, cry, get angry, feel trepidation, guilt, joy, inspiration or hope. All fiction writers, film directors and even professional speakers are taught about the emotional 'beat map' - a series of emotional highs and lows that we should take our audience through in order to capture that which is uniquely human - their emotional hearts. Without it, there would be no story and no experience, and teaching is the same.

In order to capture hearts, we don't have to go to the same degree as a blockbuster movie or a TED-style presentation when we are delivering training, but here are some suggestions that will ensure your heart-centred, soul-driven learners feel connected and engaged with your training:

1. Ensure you include learning outcomes that are focussed on the way your learners will *feel* by the end of your course and not just the skills and knowledge they will attain.
2. Ensure your course descriptions also refer to the sense of 'good' your course brings to the individual, their families, their communities and the world.
3. Use emotional language and include the world 'feel' throughout your training.

4. Find out what meaning and purpose your learners place on their lives, and refer to it throughout your training.
5. Find out how your learners feel before your training and ask them how they want to feel by the end of it, and throughout your training constantly refer to how what you are teaching is taking them to that emotional goal.
6. Include stories and case studies of real people and events in your training programs. They can be sad, funny and everything in between. Just make sure they are relevant to what you are teaching and make a learning point more meaningful.
7. Include reflective-type activities in your training, such as guided journal reflections, exploration of deeper meaning and the sharing of personal experiences in group/forum discussion.

> *Add some emotion to your training. People are more likely to remember and recall information when they've been anchored by some kind of emotion.*
> *#edupreneur @CordinerSarah*

NOURISH BOTH SIDES OF THE BRAIN

Next, we need to ensure that our learning content and delivery is cognitively engaging to both sides of our learners' brains, in particular. In order to absorb our training, our left-brain learners will subconsciously break down what we are teaching them into many parts, and our right brain learners will be pulling all of the parts together to create one whole.

Without this becoming a lesson in neuroscience, course creators and educators can improve their training delivery by understanding this difference, and although learners are never wholly 'left' or 'right', they do tend to be more dominant on one side. Therefore, delivering to only one type will automatically exclude a large portion of your learner group.

Here are some considerations to make to be inclusive to both left and right brain learners:

Left Brain Learners:

The way I like to remember who our left-brain people are, is:

"L" is for logical.

Learners who are predominantly left-brained in nature are very similar to the analytical information processing style of learning.

> *Left-brain learners are logical and need step by step instructions.*
> *#edupreneur @CordinerSarah*

Here are twelve characteristics and suggestions for engaging the left-brain learner in your online and offline training courses.

1. Be linear and sequential in your delivery
   Left-brain learners are logical and therefore like their training courses to be linear and sequential. Make sure that you have a very clear curriculum that definitively shows every module lecture, learning outcome, and criteria that will be covered.

2. Break down instructions into step processes
   Left-brain learners love step-by-step processes. For every concept, skill, principle or theory that you are teaching, try to illustrate it with a step-by-step model.

3. Includes statistics, facts and quotes
   Left-brain learners love statistics, facts, evidence and proof. The more numbers and evidence you can give to your training and every point you make, the more engaged and trusting left-brain learners will be of your training.

4. Teach and tell
   Left-brain learners are often very comfortable with didactic lecture-based training, so feel free to use this method with your left-brain learners.

5. Embed analysis
   Left-brain learners love analytical exercises and activities. For example, if you are teaching a section on industry terminology you could use crosswords or word searches. If you are teaching any kind of concept or method, you could get them to conduct a research project or analytical report that compares a number of viewpoints on the matter.

6. Include details and investigation exercises
   Left-brain learners love detail, so ensure that you provide opportunity for further reading and exploration on your subject as they are likely to want to investigate further.

7. Back yourself up
   Ensure that you reference all sources of information, facts, figures and statistics. The left-brain learner is likely to question you if you don't.

8. Stay logical
   Ensure that your lectures and training follow a logical and progressive sequence. If the left-brain learner feels like the order jumps around, they will become frustrated and disengaged with your training.

9. Schedule independent study time
   The left-brain learner often prefers to work alone so that they can break down their learning in their own way.

Sarah Cordiner

10. Keep it clean and minimalist
    Left-brain learners like things to be tidy, clean and orderly, so make sure that your classroom is tidy if you deliver face-to-face training. If your training is online, ensure that your lecture titles are clearly defined, well written, and void of spelling and grammatical errors. Not only is this good practice, but it will really irritate your left-brain learners if these errors exist.

11. Minimise distractions
    Left-brain learners like simplicity. Make sure that you have limited background noise and minimise all possible distractions in the training process. If you are delivering training online, avoid having overly distracting graphics, animations or any music in the background of your videos.

Right Brain Learners:

The right side of our brain is the visual, creative and conceptual side of us.

"The right side of our brain is the visual, creative and conceptual side of us. Feed it visual educational content in your courses". #edupreneur @CordinerSarah

Here are eight considerations and methods that you can use to engage the right-brain learner in your online and offline training courses:

1. Encourage thinking beyond the scope of the curriculum.

The right-brained part of us is the part that likes to think outside of the box and considers how the learning applies to our lives beyond the scope of the course curriculum. For example, if your course is about how to farm honey, your left-brain learners will be considering each and every small, broken down step for producing the perfect honey, whereas your right-brain learners would be more likely to be thinking about how they can cook with honey, flavour their tea with honey, or produce skincare products with honey. Instead of focussing on the constituent parts of the development process, the right-brain learner prefers to see the completed result in their mind's eye, and importantly, for what and why it was being farmed in the first place.

2. Encourage innovation.

Right-brain learners like to synthesize knowledge and create new ideas from two entirely separate pieces of information, fuelling creativity and innovation. They think inside and outside of the classroom and consistently draw upon knowledge, skills and information that they have acquired from multiple sources when making sense of new content.

3. Present multiple viewpoints.

Where left-brain learners tend to be more fixed in their own viewpoints and opinions, the right-brain learner has a natural ability to move lucidly between different perspectives as part of their creative tendency, and this is most certainly what they prefer to do in the classroom as it helps their learning process.

Activities such as debates where they have to swap sides and fight for both sides of the party are great for this. You can also encourage learners to reflect, share and discuss how they believe others might be feeling in given scenarios. Alternatively, you can encourage them to take a philosophical approach to exploring different concepts and coming up with different ideas and theories, that they neither agree nor disagree with, but regardless must explore.

4. Get visual.

Right-brain learners share many commonalities with the visual learner. This side of the brain recognises colour, shapes and imagery. So the more that we can include this in our courses, the greater the learning experience for our right-brain learners will be.

5. Stimulate the senses.

Right-brain learners love to use all of the senses when learning. They can multitask quite efficiently and do not become distracted when they are stimulated by multiple senses. They can quite happily listen, read, write, think and sing to music all at the same time.

6. Let them take their own notes.

Because right brain learners like to conceptualise, they adore the opportunity to write notes, draw diagrams and doodle while you're teaching. Engaging the right brain learner can be as simple as providing your PowerPoint slides as a handout so that they can make their own notes next to each one. They like to see how you have explained something and illustrated it, but then they want to have the opportunity to translate that into their own understanding and style.

7. Get practical.

Right-brain learners like to think aloud. Therefore providing them with opportunities to have open discussion with others can substantially support their learning. Using mind maps, spider diagrams, vision boards, post-it-note idea mapping, scrapbooks and project work in the learning process are all great ways of engaging the right-brain learner.

8. Creative problem solving.

Because right-brained learners find it easy to see the big picture, they are less likely to be bogged down in the detail of the problem, and they also find it frustrating to do so. They prefer to come up with alternative methods and solutions. If you can provide guided creative problem-solving activities in your online and offline training, this is sure to engage the right brain learner. As an example, if you teach entrepreneurship, perhaps you could give your learners a challenge where they must compete against their classmates to raise a certain amount of money within a fixed time period, starting with just $1!

THE LEARNING PRINCIPLE OF PRACTISE

Adult learners are often engaged in learning because a problem needs to be solved. Practising skills in a controlled environment allows them to grow self-efficacy in new tasks that prepare them to act autonomously outside of the learning environment. The more an adult learner can practice new skills, competencies or the application of knowledge, the more transformational impact the learning intervention will have.

Where the learn-by-doing approach is slightly more biased towards real-life, on-the-job practical training, the practise principle refers to being in a more controlled learning environment and utilising dummy, or simulated scenarios, equipment, resources and exercises.

This method is best used when there is a high-risk factor attached to practical training, or it is difficult to provide real-life practice for some reason. This approach can also give confidence to those who are nervous of going "straight into the real thing," and this fear then acts as a barrier to learning.

Some people would not follow an online course on web development if they were being asked to do it on a real or live website, especially if it was their own because then the element of perfection would simply stop them from ever finishing. But giving them a dummy website for training and practice purposes will remove this sense of fear and being overwhelmed.

Similarly, someone who is very new to the customer service

industry may not enroll in a course that will throw her straight into a role that includes facing a customer. However, she would feel much happier practising her customer service skills using role play, scenarios and pre-recorded customer complaint calls.

Some examples of how to provide safe, simulated practical training experiences for the purpose of practice are:

Virtual reality training

Virtual reality is my new favourite way of designing, developing and delivering training. This really is a game-changer for our industry as it allows learners to truly experience, practise and apply their theoretical learning and skills to situations where they may not previously have had the opportunity.

At the extreme end, imagine how many lives will be saved if frontline soldiers could have more real practise identifying, disarming and disposing of explosive ordnance, without the risk of being blown apart. Imagine how much safer our offshore oil and gas deep sea divers would be if they could have more practice doing deep rig maintenance in high swell seas, without the risk of drowning.

Imagine how much safer underground mining would be if miners could have more practice hours before risking their lives in potentially toxic air under tonnes of unstable rock. Imagine how much safer medical surgery would be if doctors could practise more surgeries before performing on you.

On the more 'every day' end of the spectrum, imagine how

many fewer trainers and employees would want to shoot themselves free of boredom and instead be stimulated and excited when it comes to going through basic workplace induction training, or workplace hazard identification, that replicates scenarios around their actual workplace using virtual reality?

Imagine if you could deliver your sales training program by putting your learners in a 'real' high pressure, unpredictable sales environment that has the artificial intelligence to respond accordingly to your own responses and reactions to the sales situation. Cool, huh?

This might all seem a bit sci-fi to some, but it's very real and very available right now, for much less than you think.

My company MainTraining has a partnership with a virtual reality tech company to enable our standard accredited and non-accredited curriculum design services to be produced in virtual reality form. With the purchase of some simple gadgets (headsets and gloves) and the download on your company computers of a piece of software that's as easy to install as a new app, we can recreate your simulated work environments, preset it with a vast array of scenarios, commands and activities that are aligned to accredited or non-accredited training outcomes that respond with artificial intelligence to the learners responses.

Before this turns into a sales pitch, be open-minded about how VR could be used in your topic to provide your learners with more opportunity for practise when it wouldn't otherwise be possible. It's not the future of education, because t's *already* here, and I strongly believe that educators who are not prepared to take on this new method of training will eventually get left behind.

Virtual reality training also allows for the benefits of immersive training with the added bonus of reducing the cost of expensive equipment, high-risk work environments, and highly specialised and expensive trainers.

> *"Take your training anywhere. Too many people assume learning is set in a formal classroom".*
> *#edupreneur @CordinerSarah*

Simulation (machines)

Simulators are last century's virtual reality, but they are very much a part of the training in today's educational landscape. Trainee pilots can use flight simulation machines before they take to the skies, mobile plant operators can practise driving heavy machinery in replica simulators before taking to the tracks, and learner drivers can practise their driving skills before hitting the public roads in a real car. Although this method is an expensive one, or requires access to a facility that has these machines in place, it is still an excellent way to embed the practise principle of adult learning.

Simulation (environment)

Not all training requires the use of machinery, but does require a learner to be familiar, autonomous and competent in certain environments. Creating a simulated environment—a controlled one as closely matched to the real life version as possible—is an effective way to bring in the practise element.

This could be as advanced creating permanent training sites, such as recreating mini-mine sites for practising mobile plant operation, or as simple as facilitating some role plays. In an online environment, you can also use this method. For example, when I am teaching online course creation I use a real learning management system for the learners to practise on, but it's not a 'live' online school, meaning that they are free to do as they please in the practising stage without causing harm to a running business. Web developers could use a real website, but not one that is representing a real business, and so on.

Case scenarios

You can use this method for both practise and contextualisation. You could teach a generic principle, and then give your learners a situation to apply their learning. A case scenario can be very complex and detailed, or very simple.

The beauty is that you can create pretend situations that directly match a situation that the learner is highly likely to experience in real life. It could be presented to them as a written story, an audio, a collection of paperwork, a video of a role play, or a video of an actual scene from real-life.

You present the scene, and then tell the learners to deal with the situation, solve the problem, or state the procedure or process they would follow next. This will test their learning and give them the opportunity to practise their new skills.

Role plays

This is simply playing out an act that may be experienced in real life. In the online space, you could encourage peer role plays via video conferencing, or get them to film themselves playing out their role with someone at home.

So long as you provide them with the scene, at least one side of the script so that the role play is guided, and a series of follow-up reflection questions to provide educational purpose to the activity, then you can get as creative with this as you like.

Projects

Depending on your topic, creating practical projects is another way to embed the practise principle of adult learning. Projects can be written, practical, video or audio, and there are endless ways you could create projects for your learners to practise what they have learned.

Ensure that the project is something that allows them to practise what they have been taught in your training and one that will show their results.

Of course, this list is not exhaustive of the different ways to help your learners practise what they have been learning in your course, but hopefully it provides you with some food for thought about the ways that you can bring practise into your training.

THE LEARNING PRINCIPLE OF PERSONAL DEVELOPMENT

"Education is not preparation for life; education is life itself". ~John Dewey

Too many people assume that learning is restricted to the formal classroom, which for many of us drags up memories that make us shudder. The truth is that we are learning 24-hours a day. Our brain is taking in billions of bits of data and information and connecting it to data it already carries every second of every day.

Every day is a school day, and we can either let our brain take in information subconsciously, or we can feed it with carefully chosen information so that we can develop ourselves in desired areas.

If we consciously feed our brains with selected information, we can become highly skilled and knowledgeable in any topic we focus our attention on absorbing information from.

As edupreneurs, it is our role to help ourselves, as well as our learners, actively and willingly seek new information on our topics so that they can master them.

Our brain capacity is never fixed. If we control what we feed our brains, we can master anything we want to.
#edupreneur @CordinerSarah

Not to mention, in the education space, personal development is often a required element of our roles as part of compliance requirements to teach and train. In Australia for example, to be a qualified Trainer Assessor, you must provide evidence of your industry currency each year in order to maintain compliance (and even your job, contracted or employed) under the regulatory body requirements. If you cannot provide substantial evidence that your skills and knowledge are fresh and up-to-date, you can expect to lose business. Similarly in the UK, there are strict requirements under LLUK to demonstrate your own professional development as an adult educator to stay employable in the industry, and rightfully so. *We* must be lifelong learners as well as enabling our learners to be.

Carol Dweck tells us that there are two major categories of lifelong learners: those who believe that our intelligence and skill sets are fixed and cannot be altered, and those that believe our skills and intelligence is malleable.

Those who think intelligence is fixed think that you are either smart, or not. They believe that if they fail a test at school, it is because they are not good at learning, and they often withdraw or resist situations that are unfamiliar to them or will require them to acquire new skills and knowledge. Their efficacy towards new tasks is low, as they innately believe that they are incapable of learning what needs to be learned. These people are very difficult to engage in any form of self-development or lifelong learning, and they often fail to engage in any form of training after formal education. Because they believe that intelligence is fixed, they believe that their skills will not improve no matter what or how you teach them.

Those who believe that intelligence is malleable, believe that our intelligence and skills can change and develop with practice and training. They are not halted by new tasks or challenges, as they know that with some training, practice and effort they can acquire and master new information. These people often remain in some form of self-development later in life and regularly engage in learning purely for the sake and enjoyment of learning. They go on to develop a plethora of new talents as they progress through life.

"The skills and knowledge you posses are directly proportionate to the amount of effort you put into obtaining them."
@CordinerSarah #edupreneur

Know their drivers

The intrinsic, personal desires and ambitions of an adult learner need to be considered when planning and delivering adult learning programs. As learners get older, their reason for participating in learning programs often moves from external drivers such as getting a promotion, to internal drivers, like simply learning for pure pleasure or interest in learning something new.

Depending on the topic that you teach and how you deliver that to your learners, exactly how you cultivate lifelong learners in your topic can vary considerably. It is driven by the learner's internal motivation, and the importance, relevance and enjoyment that mastering that topic gives them.

In the chapter, I have included some suggestions to help you enhance your own personal development habits. This is critical as an educator, so that, by default, you can select methodologies that may best suit your particular audience in your own learning programs.

PLAN FOR LIFELONG LEARNING

The kind of education that we are most familiar with is referred to as the 'front end' concept of education.

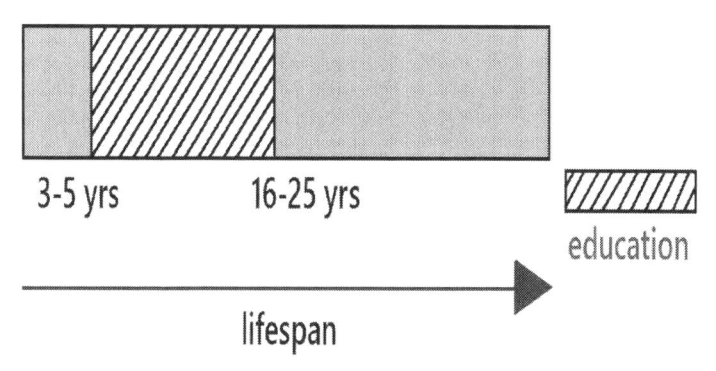

Figure 2.1 **The front-end model of education**
Source: Boyle (1982: 8)

It's called 'front-end' because this very traditional approach to education happens only at the beginning of our lives and then stops as soon as society deems us mature. We head off, presumably, into the world of work.

It refers to the formal schooling most of us receive from primary school to the end of secondary school. Coombes and Ahmed (1974) describe this formal education as a "*highly institutionalised, chronologically graded and hierarchically structured education system, spanning from lower primary to upper university.*"

Such a formal model is considered as lacking in its ability to create maximum impact by adult learning theorists such as

Jarvis and Peters (1987). It suggests that from formal schooling, people will attain knowledge and skill that is sufficient to serve them for the rest of their lives, and that intelligence and autonomy is dependent on age. Many adults would probably claim that this is simply not the case.

This front-end concept of education is one that we should avoid or minimise as much as possible in the design of our training programs, as it leaves the learning significantly incomplete, inapplicable or non-utilisable to the learner's real life. If we take away the age range, it is a very stark reality that training organisations and businesses that conduct training today still do not actively plan for any learning to continue to develop after a program of training has taken place. This makes far too many learning programs front-end with respect to job roles and even entire careers. In the transient and rapidly changing world that we live in now, this is simply unacceptable and not at all conducive to effective and continuous adult learning.

The completion of formal schooling is certainly not the end of a person's learning journey, and it is the same in adult education interventions. We must remember to design our training programs in a way that intentionally enables the learning journey to continue long after the program has ceased. Adults of all ages re-engage with some form of education in later life. Whether it is to gain necessary qualifications for a better job or for pleasure, it thus phases out this end state phenomenon.

Lifelong Learning Is the Key

"I don't think much of a man who is not wiser today than he was yesterday." ~ Abraham Lincoln

Learning should not, and does not, stop in childhood or when we leave the school classroom. It is a process that we go through, formally and informally, throughout our entire lives.

Lifelong learning considers education to be "*a process of accomplishing personal, social and professional development throughout the life-spans of individuals in order to enhance the quality of life of both individuals and their collectives*" (Dave, 1976, p.11).

Similarly, Dewey (1916) suggests that education is one of the major foundations of a rich life and should not remain solely at the beginning of life or in childhood alone. Rather, it should be situated at any stage of life and further built upon at different times. Although many businesses and learning institutions are doing a fabulous job at implementing lifelong learning, there is still the need for significant improvement.

Bring this concept to the everyday course creator, and we have a great deal of work to do to beat the shortsighted marketers 'smash out courses quick' mentality. Instead, we must shift our focus to designing courses that have lifelong impact on our students, and facilitates a desire within them to continue building upon their skills and knowledge long into their future.

> *Create lifelong learners. Learning should never stop when we leave the classroom, otherwise, we fail in more ways than one.*
> *#edupreneur @CordinerSarah*

Let's look at YOU as a lifelong learner to help with this concept.

Here are ten ways that you can become a lifelong learner:

Create a personal development plan

In the business and working world, we are (or should be) given Professional Development Plans. These are formal documents given to staff, and facilitated and monitored by management to ensure we are progressing in our job-specific skills and knowledge areas. This is because corporations know that if their staff do not continuously improve, neither does the work they do. Therefore, it stifles the growth potential and competitiveness of the business. What I find fascinating is how many of us do not apply the same principles in our personal development lives and businesses.

By focussing on the areas of our lives we would like to improve, get better at, or learn for the first time, we are ensuring that *we* do not go stale either. Do you keep a list of things you'd love to learn or master?

You can grab a free copy of a Personal Development Plan template here: www.sarahcordiner.com/PD.

Ideally, you should complete a new PDP every three months, as we change so much as our environment and circumstances change around us. I do mine once a month to ensure that I am always working to be the best version of myself.

Reading books

There is very little in this world that has not been extensively written about. Books are one of my top ways of learning new information. They help me to grow as an educator, as well as a lifelong learner. The more interactive you can make book reading, the better. According to the Cone of Learning, we only retain 5-45% of what we read. However, if we write that down and actually do something with the information we have taken in, the retention of knowledge can increase to over 50%.

Adding colour (I use highlighter pens) and post-it notes to sentences that are a key learning point for me, or stand out as something I want to remember, helps increase my information retention rates. I re-read my highlighted sentences at the end of each chapter and then write up a little summary of what I learned in a Google Doc.

Going back to the Cone of Learning, I then do something else. When we teach what we have learned, we increase our information retention to 90% or better. So I then pick out the information that applies to my audience, and I either add it to my online courses (keeping them updated), and/or add them as statuses or social media posts in my social media auto-posting tool (buffer.com) to maintain my industry presence and helpfulness.

What if you don't like reading? As a full-time business owner and mum, I always find time to read, but I know how hard it can be to keep up this discipline. I found an app that I love called 'Blinkist', which for a small monthly fee ($10 at the time of writing this) you can get a 15-minute written and audio summary of hundreds of thousands of books. It is brilliant! It sums up all of the key learning points you could possibly need to know, and while I'm grabbing some lunch, making dinner or having a quick walk during a break, I listen to a 15-minute 'blink' to get all the juice from an entire book. Lifelong learning in magic form!

Why not share the top ten things you learned from reading THIS book—in a video, a Facebook group or a blog post? I would love to know, so please do share it in my Entrepreneur to Edupreneur Facebook group when you make your report!

For your learners:

- Give them a book to read on your topic and ask them to report back to the group the top ten things they learned from the book in a discussion area.
- Get them to deliver a mini-training session or submit a video on the top five things they learned from the book.
- If you have a big group and a big book, break the learners into groups and assign each group a chapter to read and report back on the top points they learned.

Take online courses

Another favourite of mine. I am as much of a learner as I am an educator, and I strongly believe that educators of all kinds are only as good as they are learners themselves. By watching courses, we not only gather new information and new perspectives on our own topic and other complementary topics that keep our own content fresh and up-to-date, but by watching our peers, we can gather best practice tips and tricks for our own delivery and presentation.   I don't just absorb what my fellow edupreneurs are teaching. I also absorb HOW they are teaching. The way they speak, gesture, use their voice, inject their personalities and explain their craft. I also observe the way their courses have been constructed and are visually and technically presented.

Doing this regularly ensures that my own practice and programs are constantly being self-assessed for improvement and that my business and I continually grow through new learning. Never be killed by complacency. The second you stop improving, your competitors will come along and run right over you.

After taking any course, I follow the same process as I do with books. I pick out the top things I have learned and share them in every way I can to both help others and solidify my own information retention.

For your learners:

1. Take all the courses that you possibly can in your own topic area (especially if you think you know it all), as

well as complementary courses to your field of expertise.

2. Recommend the courses you love to your students. This doesn't take anything away from you if your courses are better, and they have already paid to be on your course! Think of it like the recommended reading pages you get on any course or formal education you might join.

3. You can take this course referral to another level by creating affiliate links for yourself so that the very act of recommending them earns you referral commissions too. It's very easy to do this with platforms like Udemy, where you can set up a 'clickbank' account (www.clickbank.com). Take the link from any Udemy course you want to recommend, and it will then produce an affiliate link for you. You can make up to 50% of the sale price if one of your learners takes that recommended course. Many online instructors have affiliate referral programs too – I personally pay 50% of every sale to my affiliates and am always looking for more affiliates.

4. Similarly with the book method, you could get your learners to report back in the group discussion or file sharing areas with the top ten things they learn from the course they took.

Create a 'stuff to learn' folder

Emails

I am often sent emails from mailing lists that I've signed up to that have really useful articles or downloads that I want to learn later. So I have a folder in my email inbox called 'stuff to learn'. I drop all non-urgent things I'd like to absorb later into that folder and then come back to it on my scheduled 'PD' days

The shared folder

Create a shared resources library for you and your students. A shared Google Drive folder is great for this, or even the files tab inside Facebook groups where anyone can add content and files or links that they come across that might help the personal development of the other group members. Not only do I do this for my students, but I also do it with my inner circle edupreneurs so that we can all learn together. Whenever any of us come across something helpful to our roles and topics, we drop it in the shared folder so that we can all benefit from a professional development library collective!

Go to conferences

I'm a bit of a conference junkie, and I attend them frequently. Even if I'm a speaker, I often stay for the whole event and learn as much as I can from my peers. Register yourself on the conference directory websites and create a personalised notification for conference topics that you are interested in. You will get email notifications whenever conferences with that theme in the countries you selected are announced. This will allow you to take a few days out of every month or two to dedicate time to your own self-development from the best in your industry. It's a great way to ensure that you are staying abreast of up-to-date and trending information and best practises in your industry. It has the added bonus of exposure and networking.

As with books and online courses, I also record all of my top tips and learnings and turn them into education for others.

For your learners:

- Get them to find and list ten conferences and/or expos in their local or country that could contribute to their own professional development
- Get them to share the top learnings or written notes from any conference that they attend

Strategically build a circle of influence

I have learned more from the people that I hang around (virtually and in person) than I think I ever did in formal education. It is said through theories of 'the power of proximity' that we become a replica of those that we spend most of our time around.

I actually tried this out once and can absolutely attest to the power of this. I had wanted to be an author for a good fifteen years before I published my first book. The reason I hadn't published one in that time had nothing to do with my writing ability. I have always been a skilled and passionate writer, and I had hundreds of thousands of words going stale in my hard drive. In fact, most of the words in this book had been rotting away on a hard drive for a good seven years before they made it to this page.

For some reason I felt like authors were these almost mythical, untouchable, pedestalled creatures that had epically magical powers and humongous marketing teams and budgets behind them. Something I didn't have. I also knew very little about the world of publishing, and therefore I simply assumed it was impossible, or at the very least, required a highly intelligent and spectacularly overpaid publicist to make it happen for me.

Years went by as I occasionally picked up that hard drive in the bottom of my office drawer when looking for paperclips. Then, I discovered Facebook groups. More importantly, I discovered Facebook groups for authors. I joined every single one I could find. I asked questions and joined in on conversations. I MADE FRIENDS with as many of them as I could, and essentially, I immersed myself in authorship and surrounded myself with authors.

I discovered two major things:

a) Authors were exactly like me except they had taken their books off their hard drives.
b) It really wasn't that hard to press 'upload' to Amazon.

Another thing I realised was that now I was surrounded by thousands of people who had published books, publishing books seemed like the normal, everyday thing to do. It was the new "*everybody's doing it*" thing, and therefore, it didn't seem so out of reach or abnormal anymore. Of course, not everybody is writing a book, but when you are surrounded by people who are, it feels that way, and it makes following the crowd a little easier.

After a month or so of hanging out in these groups, I realised that I had everything all of my new author friends had. I was travelling to India to speak at a conference, and only three months away from giving birth to my first child. It was also my 30th birthday that very same weekend. I decided to take a few days off after the conference and dedicate them to getting a book published.

I wrote, published and got my first book, *Maximising Staff Training on a Minimum Budget,* to Amazon Number 1 within 72 hours. This only happened because by being around authors, the authorship habits and practices rubbed off onto me, and I saw myself as similar to these people.

Have you analysed your circle of influence lately? Whom do you want to be like? What skills, position, physical appearance or qualities do you want? Are the people in your immediate circle and daily life in alignment with that? If not, you need to move circles with urgency.

For your learners:

- Get them to find and join at least ten communities that are filled with people who they want to be like or have what they want to have.
- Get them to do an analysis of their current circle of influence to see if and how they need to adjust their daily influences.

Reflection

I discussed this in more detail in a separate chapter, but I felt it was important to reinforce the importance of self-reflection in our personal development practices. Simply absorbing and regurgitating other people's information is not enough to truly be a great educator. If we are to lead with strength, authority and difference, we need to master our own informed perspectives.

Just as the relevance principle of adult learning says, we will be far more motivated by our development and retain the information for longer if we take the time to apply what we have learned to our own realities.

By journaling, discussing or tying up what you have learned and what it means to you, how it applies to your life, how it can inform your own practice, how it has challenged your existing ways of thinking or added a new dimension to what you already knew, you will significantly expand your knowledge base and optimise your professional development practices.

Teach

As mentioned in the previous tips, when we teach, we retain more information. We synthesise its application to our own world and we help others at the same time.

Whenever I read a book, take a course, attend an event, read an article or pick something up in a Facebook group, I always do so with both my learner *and* teacher hats on. I always think to myself "*How and in what context could I teach this to others? How could I pass this onto others in my field?"*

Without failure, almost everything I learn ends up as either an online course tutorial video, a YouTube video, a book chapter, a blog or guest article, a social media tip or a Facebook live stream video.

I even encourage my Edupreneurs to do the same for their own learning, their learners and for the benefit of contributing to their industry, or their own omnipresence and credibility. Go to my edupreneur group '*Entrepreneur to Edupreneur – Course Creators'* and inside the group search box look for the hashtag '#30days30tips.' You'll see how I used this method to help my own learners grow.

Sign up to industry magazines and blogs

There are some fabulous blogs and industry specific magazines out there, and I'd bet my last glass of wine that there is one for a topic that you are passionate about learning more about. Simply list all the keywords for the topic you wish to learn about, and then type in [blog] next to each one in a Google search. For example, if I want to learn about e-learning, I would type into Google: "e-Learning [blog]" and this will bring up all of the blogs with this keyword. Then you can simply check through each result and sign up to the mailing lists or RSS feeds of the ones that look the most interesting to you.

To add to this, you can similarly sign up for Google alerts for all of the keywords you wish to learn about, and Google will send you notifications whenever articles are published on that topic so that you can keep up-to-date without any effort whatsoever.

For your learners:

- Get them to list all of the keywords for the topics they want to learn about, and get them to sign up to three industry blogs and create, at least, three Google alerts.

Use life experiences as opportunities to grow

Often our challenges and struggles are our real teachers. Those who see challenges as opportunities to learn and grow are more successful, wealthier and happier than those who see challenges as unfair and cruel events made for a period of self-pity. Lifelong learners come from a place of mastery where they assess what can be gained from the experience.

Practice for you and your learners:

Create a timeline of all the major events in your life, good and bad. Then ask yourself "*If life was a teacher, what has it been trying to teach me all this time?*"

For each individual event, then ask:

- What is this teaching me?
- What lesson does this bring?
- What positive things was I supposed to learn from this?
- What can I learn about myself from this?
- What can I learn about the world around me from

this?
- How has this positively impacted my life?

Having read these questions, what activities and strategies could you bring into your training programs to ensure that you are fostering lifelong learning in your students?

LIFELONG LEARNING IN THE WORKPLACE

For those course creators working in organisations, or creating their training programs for a workplace environment, here are some checklist items to bring more lifelong learning into your training.

- ☐ Are all job roles within the organisation aligned to a job competency profile that outlines the required and desired skills, competencies and affective qualities of the role, and do these match to appropriate standard and optional training and education specifications and career pathway plans? How will your course fit into the overall career progression pathway of the employees?

- ☐ Is an individual's progress and implementation of new skills and competencies, attitudes and behaviours monitored and recorded regularly in a 360 degree manner, by the training provider(s), the business and the learner themselves?

- ☐ Do you liaise with your clients and/or training providers (depending on which side you work in) around these competency and career pathway plans so that training can be designed accordingly?

- ☐ Is training designed in a way that encourages further and progressive implementation of skills and knowledge after the formal element of the training has ceased?

- How will your program encourage learning to continue long after the course has been completed, and how will this be tracked and monitored?

Make sure that lifelong learning has significant opportunity to take place by incorporating the design and development of training into company strategic objectives, industry needs and long-term career pathway plans. It not only saves repetition of learning and teaching, but it also saves on time and expense. It makes the learner feel valued and clear about their development journey. They can clearly see their progression, which fuels motivation and self-worth.

At MainTraining we have conducted workforce planning, career pathway planning and competency profiling for many organisations, including fortune 500 companies, ASX listed companies and one of the largest oil and gas construction projects in the Southern hemisphere. By consulting with industry leaders and conducting vigourous research into various industry learning opportunities and practices, we were able to standardise the compulsory, compliance and desired training processes for over one hundred different construction site job roles. This resulted in a streamlined HR process, skills retention, lower staff turnover, reduced costs in repeated training and a much greater business-wide commitment to people development in an industry that regularly experiences skills shortages.

By planning for learning interventions with a lifelong

perspective, we are contributing to the optimum development of an individual and to the economy of the country, which their skills enable.

ACTIVITY: Plan for Lifelong Learning

- How will you ensure that learning will continue after your training program has taken place?

- How can you phase out the 'front end' approaches to learning in your environment?

- What does lifelong learning mean to you?

- How does your training institution or business encourage lifelong learning?

- How could your learners or staff be better informed and provided with opportunities about lifelong learning?

THE LEARNING PRINCIPLE OF BEHAVIOURISM

Have you ever been in a situation in your past where the teacher said something along the lines of "*Everyone else has achieved xyz, so why haven't you?*" or "*Everyone else seems to understand xyz, so why don't you?*"

Yep, most of us have, and it hurts like a kick in the genitalia.

In the modern day world of planning, designing and delivering training, we must ensure that our training is free of the cause-effect assumption. What I mean by this is that we are not assuming that by delivering a certain curriculum, all learners will come out perfectly, or equally manufactured. This would be called a behaviorist's way of thinking, and it can be extremely detrimental to the learning experiences of some (never to the ones who are coming out on top, but very much to the ones who are an anomaly to the overall average).

When I got my first teaching post in the UK, my first major project was to design, develop and deliver a national training program for long-term unemployed single mothers. The laws had recently changed as to whether you could continue to receive government welfare payments or if you had to be forced back to work based on the age of your youngest child. Due to a relaxed single parent payout system in the UK, many single mums had been making a very generous income from the welfare state by simply having more kids. Suddenly, they had to go and get a job - something that most of my students had never done in their adult lives.

So I had to develop a series of training programs to help them achieve this outcome. Being that it was a government-funded initiative, there was heavy monitoring and measuring criteria attached to my contract.

But here was my first problem:

My overall objective: get them into work.

The Government's assumption: Give them a class on job hunting, and they'll all get a job.

Clearly, this was not a situation where one intervention would get the same results for everyone. One size fits none.

We simply cannot presume that a single course, however good it may be, will result in every participant coming out with a job.

I was stuck in a behaviourist trap. If my students didn't get work, the criteria by which this scheme was assessed would deem my program as ineffective at best and a waste of taxpayers' money at worst. Not to mention what it would do to the efficacy of the women in the program who did not 'fit the production line requirements.'

I was up against the national government, a hopeless model and dismal statistics. So here's what I did.

First, I conducted some (albeit novice) research on what the major barriers to employment were for this general population as a whole. I also directly asked them what they felt was holding them back most and keeping them from moving towards employment.

What came back was interesting and gave me enough evidence to convince my boss (mentioned in the dedication of this book) to let me do things a little differently. She reminded me that we had a government objective to meet, and then she looked at me with complete belief in her eyes and said, "*Go for it.*"

Now the pressure was really on! Letting the Government down was one thing, letting my students down another, but letting down someone who clearly had absolute faith in my abilities was something I wasn't going to let happen.

I got to work and designed multiple programs that crossed everything from addressing the internal belief systems my learners had, to the practical skills required to find and keep a job. Then I designed them to stand alone, but they could also be progressively walked through for those most in need of one whole unit of training.

Then, I had to address the Government's need for quantitative data. My problem was that much of what we were teaching was the development of soft skills, feelings, attitudes and less tangible or measurable outcomes. I was playing in behaviourist land so they needed data. Then it came to me. To please the suits, I could make qualitative and seemingly immeasurable student progress quantitative data.

I designed ipsative assessments for all courses. What are ipsative assessments? They are the strategy for measuring each individual's progress from their own individual starting point.

Why? Because we are all too different to assess personal growth in a means tested or cohort benchmarking manner, especially in the context in which I was teaching. For some of the women I was working with, simply getting dressed and physically arriving to the workshop was monumental progress in their life. The level of anxiety they suffered meant that this simple act would have been entirely insignificant to a measure of getting a job, a criteria that would have made this woman feel like a failure and subsequently have her confidence knocked down even further. Whereas, to her, it was the single biggest achievement of the last five years of her life, and that should be celebrated.

To others, the same size achievement may have been learning how to write their CV on the computer, or to another, getting a senior manager's role at the local hotel.

Humans cannot always be put into boxes and measured equally against predefined criteria. The effort one takes to achieve something small may be far more effort than another person puts in to achieve something huge.

With this in mind, my multiple series of training courses and ipsative assessment methods went on to win an award in people development. I was twenty-one years old, and I was getting 100% satisfaction rates and over 76% of my participants were moving into fulltime employment or formal education immediately from my workshops. For most of my learners, it was the first time they had worked in their lives.

Therefore, had I allowed my training to remain in the behaviourist's model, this result would not have happened. My participants would have felt judged. They would have failed and felt that they were not good enough. In this instance, the behaviourist model of 'one size fits all' and 'cause equals effect' would have been a disastrous approach.

As educators, it is important for us to remember that while we are drowning in compliance and systems, people are not machines. Therefore, regardless of how well we teach, learners differ in how much they take in and how quickly they can independently execute new skills safely and efficiently without supervision.

Assuming that a single learning experience will affect everyone the same way is the same as enrolling twenty people on the same driver-learning program and expecting them all to perform with identical driving abilities on test day. Far too many variables can affect this, and therefore we must factor in sufficient review, assessment and flexibility of delivery.

We have to ensure that we have processes and procedures in place to consistently check in on the attainment, retention and application of the new knowledge, skills and competencies we are providing to our learners. According to Dewey (1938), behaviourists suggest that learning is isolated to the individual, and that what and how much is learned is determined solely by the learner and the training they are put under. Behaviourist John Watson believed that outside influences were irrelevant to the outcomes of learning and teaching, seeing all children (his definition of learners) as the "ultimate blank slate." I personally think Watson must have been a massive douche.

He claimed that behaviourist principles could be used to mould children into any kind of specialist, regardless of their nature and the world that they lived in. While this example may seem extreme, even in our modern world we still see this approach to adult education and training every day.

Many training programs are still designed without being learner-centered, without the context and conditions of the learning environment truly being taken into consideration, and the previous experiences, attitudes, preconceptions and existing skill-set being analysed in advance. Yet we still expect our learning recipe to regurgitate out the same result for every student.

And if it doesn't? A trainer who has a behaviourist approach to their training would believe that if a student failed, it is because he didn't try hard enough or because he had a bad attitude towards the learning program. In essence, that he didn't behave in accordance with the rules and expectations of the prescribed design. The behaviourist approach does not consider that any outside influences, such as the environment in which the learning takes place, or that the people that instruct or surround the learning can also influence any educational or developmental process, which they all do.

I must also note that the behaviourist approach to learning must not be rejected in full, as it certainly has a place in certain forms of education.

As Pavlov taught dogs to automatically salivate every time a bell rang by repetitively ringing a bell when they were fed, behaviourist approaches to learning, and even un-learning, are very effective when it comes to delivering military or pilot training, for example, or training personnel who will be working in unpredictable or dangerous environments, in overcoming phobias, or even when children are learning about the everyday dangers around them. It works by training the mind to associate a certain stimulus with a certain response.

Fortunately, the everyday adult learning environment does not require this kind of conditioning, and due to its psychological anchoring, it is best avoided to this degree unless you are qualified in such practices. However, in today's world, we can still take some benefits from the behaviourist approach to enhance adult learning programs.

What we can learn from behaviorism:

There is a positive side to the behaviourist approach to adult learning, and we can effectively use this in both face-to-face and e-learning to significantly enhance the learning experience.

Since the behaviourist approach is about producing a set result, it is very effective when used in both formative (assessing learning at key points as we go through the program) and summative assessment (assessing learning at the end of a program of study).

This approach is not just good for assessment. It can also be used as a learning and teaching methodology.

Although the behaviourists approach is often criticised as being 'old school', educators actually still use it every single day. All learning programs should have clearly defined learning outcomes, and of course, the method of training and assessing whether or not these have been acquired or achieved by the learner must be carefully selected, based on a number of considerations detailed throughout this book.

In many cases, to ascertain whether the learner has acquired these skills, we need to check via a test, activity or demonstration from the learner, all of which are pretty behaviourist in nature as they all are assessing whether or not a cause has created an effect.

As an example, 'linking and sequencing' is one way that you can use a behaviourists approach to teaching, learning and assessment in an advantageous manner:

Linking or Sequencing

Many training programs require a learner to memorise and perform set sequences of events, such as workplace procedures, task steps or a method—basically anything that requires a chain of events where the steps to be taken are predetermined and sequential in order.

If training is face-to-face, we can literally assess the learner's performance of such processes via a practical or observational assessment. When online, this could be a submission of a video or a drag-and-drop feature that requires the learner to reorder the stages of a sequence of steps by dropping each one in the right place.

ACTIVITY: Benefit from Behaviourism

1. In what ways is the behaviourist approach to learning in your educational environment a benefit to your learning journey and outcomes?

2. How does the behaviourist approach to learning limit or risk the effectiveness of training and education in your environment?

3. In light of these pros and cons, what improvements would you suggest to the learning practices in your context?

THE LEARNING PRINCIPLE OF CONSTRUCTIVISM

This theory of adult learning combines some of the ideas of experiential learning, reflective learning and student-centered learning. It is about how, as adults, we construct our knowledge and skills by experiencing them, reflecting on our experiences and then forming new ideas, skills and knowledge as a result of the amalgamation of new and old, but with a shifted perspective.

This theory explains that our understanding of any new experience, situation or information is first processed by our brains by drawing upon our previous experiences and preexisting knowledge to see if we already possess what we need to know. If our brain identifies any difference whatsoever in the new information from the old information, then we begin to decide whether the old information we have is still relevant, whether it should be discarded, or if the new information is correct or not. The theory of constructivism suggests that we are active creators of our knowledge and that a key strategy for learning to happen is to ensure that we can ask questions internally or with others, that we can "place many different hats" on it, explore and assess what we know and whether it is valuable information to retain or not.

To encourage constructivism in your classroom or training program:

- Use active learning and teaching techniques such as experiments, real-life problem solving, practical

projects and scenarios based training.
- Use facilitated reflective exercises that both give the learner the opportunity to privately explore their thoughts, and then share them with others.
- Use questioning techniques to challenge learners' preexisting perspectives and opinions, and encourage alternative viewpoints, applications or approaches.
- Continuously push them to explore and share how their perspective, understanding or knowledge is changing.
- Create expert learners by getting them to 'learn about learning', to learn HOW they are learning and acknowledge that there is development taking place. Constructivism is as much about teaching learners how to consciously learn, as it is about getting them to learn a subject's specific skill.
- Revisit similar skills and experiences often. The more we experience a certain situation and become familiar with it, the stronger our abilities and knowledge become in that experience, and therefore the more complex variations, additions and new information we can start adding to the mix each time.
- Act as the continued facilitator of these reinforcing thinking processes, but do so in a way that still draws upon your own expert source of expertise.

PART TWO

PRE-PLANNING FOR YOUR COURSE CREATION

INTRODUCTION

Preparation is the key to success. Although many course creators like to get stuck in creating and giving, there are a few more stages of pre-preparation that will help us ensure that we are building an effective online course.

In my book '*Entrepreneur to Edupreneur*', I go into the practical of *how* to create an online course, but this initial stage is about what comes before we put pen to paper, or 'pen to pixel' if we're going online!

Before we start creating our course, we need to be very clear about some key fundamentals first.

- What is the purpose of our learning program?
- Who is our target group of learners?
- What are the macro and micro needs of our learners?
- What are our learners going to get from our course?
- How will we impart our knowledge and deliver the learning outcomes?
- How will we measure progress and assess our learners' development?

This is by no means an exhaustive list of the things we need to do and plan for, but these are some of the most critical pre-planning questions to answer. In the rest of this book, we will go over these in more detail to ensure that you have all of the underpinning elements in place before you start building.

THE LEARNING PRINCIPLE OF INVOLVEMENT

Effective adult learning programs have planned for learner feedback and consultation. Adults need to feel as though they have a sense of responsibility, control and decision-making over their learning.

They need to be involved in the planning, evaluation and consultation of their own learning process to be fully on board with its successful execution. In terms of education, this requires the flexibility of the learning situation and the learning program, and most importantly, the educator must actively involve the participant in a way that allows them to have a degree of control over what they do, or, in fact, how much they learn.

In this book, we will have a look at the basics of what these principles mean for the learner and the educator, and the overall considerations that need to be made in order to prepare an effective learning program.

Involve Your Learners in the Course Design Process

One of the best ways to ensure an adult learner is going to engage in your training program is to give them the opportunity to feel as though they have had some degree of control over the design and development process. This makes them invested in the course and allows them to have a much clearer vision of its purpose and potential results. When adult learners know what they are getting, why they are getting it and feel like they own it, engagement is significantly increased.

While this book does not go into the processes and models of curriculum design, understanding your adult learner and designing effective training programs to meet their needs does require asking very similar questions to those we would ask in the formal curriculum design process. Importantly, it involves asking THEM, if you want the best results.

Using simple survey tools such as Google Forms is a great way to involve your learners in the course design process and is a method I use when I develop all of my training programs.

First, I identify WHO my learners actually are.

- What are their job titles?
- What roles do they play in their life?
- How do they identify themselves?
- Where do they live?
- What interests do they have?
- What questions do they want the answers to?

Then I ask myself what Facebook groups, LinkedIn groups or online forums might they belong to, and then I join those groups and forums.

Now you are in groups filled with your target audience. All you have to do is ASK them what they want to learn. The first time I do this I keep the question very open. I do not want to sway the results by directing them towards certain answers. All I want to do at this stage is get very general qualitative and open answers about the main topics my audience would like to learn about.

After I have gathered a list of very open and general topics my audience would like to learn, I then gather more detailed responses to better construct a formal curriculum plan.

Collect all of the general topics that have been suggested by your potential students, and then list them as either specific learning objectives or key learning topics. Then create a simple likert scale survey (a rating scale) so that your learners can rate *how much* they want to learn about each topic or proposed outcome, from 1 to 5, where 1 is "*I don't want to learn about this at all*" and 5 is "*I really want to learn about this.*"

This is when the magic really starts to happen, as now not only do the (potential) learners feel like they are part of the course, but they have also done the work for you AND, by default, given you an indication of the market value of your proposed course topic!

Here is an example of one of my likert scale surveys which I used when researching the content for my book '*Entrepreneur to Edupreneur*': www.sarahcordiner.com/BookSurvey

When we know for whom we are building our course, why we are building it for them and what it will do for them, we are laying the foundations for a highly engaging and successful learning program. And there is no better expert on your learners than the learners themselves.

It's All About Them

When we are planning effective adult learning programs, we must consider the following set of questions, and then take these questions to our marketplace:

- What, why, when, where, how, who? (discussed later)
- What skills and competencies will the students acquire?
- Are there any required outcomes or standards to be met, such as certain conditions for accreditation?
- What attitudes and behaviours do we want our students to have by the end of the course?
- What cultural or industry-specific norms, values and ethics do we want to instill?
- What are the specific learning outcomes of our learning program?
- What materials and resources are required to deliver our training?
- What will be the timing, duration and sequence of our learning program?

By asking these questions, we will be both constructing a curriculum plan as well as meeting the majority of the fundamental principles of adult learning.

Too often in the course creation process, we can too easily skew learning outcomes to the topics WE prefer to teach, or are personally more comfortable with, instead of focussing on our learners and what they need. In constructing effective adult learning programs, we must continuously remind ourselves to put our adult learners first.

With your learner in the centre of your course plans, now

answer the following questions:

WHY... Are you running this course?
Should your learners learn this?
Are you teaching this?

WHAT... Will you teach?
Will they be able to do, know and feel by the end of your course?
Methods will you use to deliver the training?
Assessment methods will you use?
Will be the benefits of them taking this course?
Makes you the best instructor for this course?

WHEN... Will it start and finish?
Can students enroll?
Will they be assessed?
Will they get feedback from the instructor?

HOW... Will it be accessed by learners?
Will it be delivered?
Will it be assessed?
Will you measure skill development and competence?
Will you make sure it meets adult principles of learning?
Will you make sure that it is inclusive and meets all learning styles and preferences?

WHO... Are the students?
Who are the educators?
Who are all of the other stakeholders?
Who are the subject matter experts?

Who will analyse the effectiveness of the program?

DEFINE YOUR TARGET GROUP

When it comes to planning and designing effective adult learning programs, it is important that we clearly understand who our target group of adult learners are so that we can design the training to meet the group needs. Later we will discuss their individual needs too.

When it comes to thinking about your target group, it is important to remember that different learners have very different characteristics. They have very different learning preferences, learning modes and learning styles. They work and live in very different environments and come from very different backgrounds, which means that the way we have to design and deliver our training needs to be very different from group to group, as well as down to an individual level as far as it is possible.

Here is a list of differentiating factors you need to consider when it comes to planning your training, how it's going to be written and how it's going to be delivered to ensure that you are meeting the basic principles of adult learning and forming the basis of an effective learning program.

Factor 1: The level and breadth of their previous work experience

Understanding your learner's previous vocational work or industry experience in the subject you are teaching is a critical element of planning and preparing your adult learning program. For example, if the majority of your target learner group has significant work experience in the topic that you are teaching then you may be able to skip more of the fundamental elements of that training and either condense the program into an intensive version, or focus the content on a much more advanced level.

Factor 2: The level and previous experiences of their formal education

What kind of formal and informal educational background does your group of learners have? What is their current skill level in the topic that you're teaching? Do they enjoy personal and professional development, or loath it based on their previous experiences? By conducting a thorough pre-assessment on all learners, what you discover about their educational background can have a profound influence on your overall training design and delivery.

Factor 3: Their Socioeconomic Background

What socioeconomic background have they come from? Are there any generalisations or stereotypes that you need to consider adding in or taking out of your learning programs depending on the type of group that you actually have? The socioeconomic status of your learners can impact everything— from the language you use, case scenario examples you use, the activities you use, your contextualisation and even the images in your presentation materials and handouts.

Factor 4: Their cultural background and needs

The cultural background that your target group of learners comes from is also a very important consideration. Let me share a real course creation story that can be seen as humorous, but in fact, is a very serious example of how the smallest things can make a huge difference to a training program's success or monumental failure.

In 2014, my company MainTraining was contracted to develop a range of qualifications for the Saudi Arabian military. Due to the technical nature of the training content, we had to employ various subject matter experts to produce the content for the specialised training. It was our job to then review that content against the national training framework specifications and ensure the design met the client style guides.

As part of the review process for one of the qualifications, we were analysing the content of a PowerPoint for a leadership module when we discovered a number of serious faux pas! One of the clip art images used to represent leadership depicted a group of black stick men all holding a platform above their heads, on top of which was a white stick man pointing the direction in which he should be carried. In a later slide, there was a stock image of half-dressed women in a shower, and in another slide was an image of a female giving orders to a group of men.

All of these were standard stock images and clipart files that in some cultures would be considered entirely unremarkable. However, when consideration is made to the specific group of learners that this training was being designed for, all of a sudden the context makes these images highly offensive and completely inappropriate.

This is a very real story, and I hope it illustrates just how important it is to consider the cultural background of your learners when designing and delivering effective adult learning programs.

Factor 5: Their age and gender

This is an obvious consideration and does not warrant much explanation. Make sure that your pre-assessment process captures the age and gender of your students so that you can ensure that your training content and program is designed to meet these differences.

For example, your training delivery for a course that will have only 18 to 21 year olds is likely to be considerably different to the same course of entirely 50+ year olds. Similarly, if you have a group of learners of a completely mixed age range, then your training content and delivery for the same course may again include very different approaches to the design and delivery.

Factor 6: Special educational needs

Designing effective adult learning programs also requires you to make special adjustments to meet special educational needs. Such adjustments could include making fonts larger, having handouts on different coloured paper, wearing hearing aid microphones, having a translator or support teacher present, among many other SEN considerations.

Factor 7: Their motivations for learning

What are their motivations for actually being in your course in the first place? If you can take the time to understand why your group is likely to be in your learning program at all, it will help you design the language in a way that continuously reinforces their motivations for being there.

Factor 8: Their language literacy and numeracy needs

We all have different skills and abilities when it comes to the technical and industry specific language of our course topics, as well as our general reading, writing, speaking, learning and numeric skills sets. By understanding where our learners sit on the language, literacy and numeracy (LLN) scale, we can better design and deliver our training to not only ensure that they are not excluded by their LLN skills but actually improve and build upon them by default through the teaching and learning activities you have selected. As an example, in my *#LevelUp Challenge* which is all about how to grow your business in 4 weeks, one of the weekly activities is to calculate the percentage growth of each of the target growth areas in their businesses. This is an obvious inclusion of math in my business development training. If you were teaching retail, the inclusion of calculating simple addition and subtraction in the form of role playing the cash till operation and money handling.

Factor 9: Their learning styles, modes and preferences

This is probably one of the more well-known concepts of developing training that meets adult learning needs. When we consider the way that our learners prefer to learn, their most natural styles of acquiring new knowledge and skills, and the modality within which they take on the greatest amount of learning, then we can be sure that we are developing effective adult learning programs. I go into this in much more detail in my online course the *Advanced Train the Trainer and Curriculum Design* course.

Factor 10: Special Program Conditions

This refers to whether your learners have qualified specifically for your training program under special conditions such as a specific funding model, unemployment status, residency status or disability status. This means that your training program may have to be designed around specific criteria, learning outcomes, performance elements, and very specific data and evidence of competence.

In essence, the list of considerations that must be made when designing and developing effective adult learning programs could be endless. However, the above list of ten key influencing factors will most certainly ensure that you have an extremely fair chance of getting it right.

ACCREDITED OR NON-ACCREDITED?

There are two kinds of learning programs: accredited and non-accredited.

Accredited programs are courses and learning that have been approved by a regulatory training body to carry credits or points towards nationally or internationally recognised qualifications, units of competency or skill sets. You have to be a registered training organisation or legally partnered with one, as well as formally qualified and experienced in your topic, in order to be able to train and assess any accredited training.

Non-accredited training can be delivered by anyone, essentially. If you have knowledge in your head, if you have expertise or some kind of skill to pass on to anyone, you can deliver training.

Any kind of training can be built under this space without having to go through regulatory or quality assurance checks, or without the trainer having to hold any qualifications.

Sarah Cordiner

IDENTIFY THE PURPOSE OF YOUR LEARNING PROGRAM

What is the purpose of your program? What are you ultimately trying to achieve for your learners?

There are four major areas of influence we can focus on when delivering training. We can aim to improve just one area, or any combination of them in our training.

1. Skills - What will they able to DO by the end of your course?
2. Knowledge - What will they know by the end of your course?
3. Attitude - What will they feel by the end of your course?
4. Behaviour - How will they act by the end of your course?

Before we start designing, developing or delivering any form of training, we first need to be clear about the purpose of that learning program. All learning programs should be designed in a way that will enhance the learners' knowledge, skills, competencies, attitudes, behaviours or feelings in some way.

Which of these core purposes your course focusses on will significantly impact not only what you teach, but how you teach it. It is imperative therefore that you decide this before putting pen to paper in your course creation stage.

In digging deeper into the pre-preparation of our course creation, this is the *'Five Bums on a Seat'* method for really drilling down into your course purpose.

The bums are the five 'W' questions we should ask ourselves, and the seat is the 'H' question we need to ask ourselves before we get started on our course creation.

- Who?
- What?
- When?
- Where?
- Why?
- How?

Ask yourself as many different versions of these questions about your learners and your course as you possibly can to really uncover the purpose.

ACTIVITY: The Purpose of Your Program

Here are some further questions to help get your thinking and direction down-pat before the course creation phase:

1. What is the title of your learning program?

2. What is the sub-title of your learning program?

3. Who are your learners?

4. Write a brief description of your learning program, giving an overview of the results it will bring to your learners.

　Use the following format to get your direction clear:

　This course, *<insert title>,* is aimed at *<describe your ideal learner>.* By the end of this course, you will *<list what they will be able to do, know and feel by the end>*.

5. How will you know that your learners have achieved those things?

THE DIFFERENT DIMENSIONS OF COMPETENCE

Having competence means having the ability to consistently perform a task to the standard of performance expected or required in the applicable context. As a trainer or course creator, it is your job to ensure that your training makes that happen.

There are Four Dimensions of Competency:

1. Individually isolated tasks
2. Managing a range of different tasks at once
3. Responding to contingencies
4. Dealing with workplace/role specific tasks

Competence is providing a student with the skills and knowledge necessary to conduct certain tasks independently, confidently, safely and autonomously, whether it's for the workplace or for their own personal wants and desires.

Before you start creating your course, consider which of these dimensions of competency your course will be addressing and to what extent they will be addressed.

Task Skills

This is the most elementary of competency development stages, and regards the ability of your learner to correctly conduct a specific, stand-alone task. As an example, this might be making a cup of tea. Often, competency based training will start with breaking down all of the individual tasks and developing learners' skills in isolated tasks, one by one, without any connection to other tasks.

Task Management Skills

Once a learner has mastered isolated skills, the next stage is to start putting those together to complete whole activities. A learner has task management skills when they are competent enough to manage and execute a combination of tasks at the same time.

An example of this could be that the learner has to make a cup of tea, a plate of toast and serve it to a customer. Essentially, here we have three major tasks that have combined to make one activity: serving breakfast to a customer.

Task Contingency Skills

This is a more complex level of competency where a learner demonstrates that they are able to respond efficiently to unexpected events while conducting a task or a combination of tasks.

This goes beyond replicating a memorised process, and it requires the learner to draw upon creative problem solving skills, transferable skills and knowledge they may have acquired elsewhere. When a learner can sufficiently demonstrate that they can manage and overcome unexpected scenarios in the tasks, they are moving from being a learner, to being an independent and competent practitioner.

In our making breakfast example, this might be seeing if the learner manages to complete the task if the kettle breaks. Would they quit the task, or know that they could boil the water in a pan on the stove, for instance? What would they do if there was no sugar left and a customer ordered sweet tea? Would the learner offer an alternative such as honey?

This level of competence is where you are providing your learners with the ability to apply their knowledge from one context to another and under unexpected circumstances.

Role Specific Skills

The fourth dimension of competency is the 'job role' or 'job environment' skill. This is when the learner can conduct a particular task, or combination of tasks, in a very specific type of environment.

In this instance, I will use a different example. Let's say the task is to answer the telephone effectively. We've all learned how to answer the telephone, as we've been doing it our whole lives. However, the way we answer the telephone will change from context to context.

The script you have to follow to answer the phone in 'Call Centre A' is going to be very different from the script you would use to answer the phone in Call Centre B.'

A mobile machine operator may have been driving excavators for ten years. However, if he switches jobs or his current company upgrades the equipment and he has to drive a new model excavator, the switches and levers might be in different places. The track, safety checks and road signs in that new location might be different, and so on.

Sarah Cordiner

Therefore, the role specific dimension of competency is all about applying a practised skill to a specific context or circumstance to safely, efficiently and compliantly conduct work tasks in alignment with local norms, culture, regulation and procedures.

Before you start creating your course, carefully consider which of the above dimensions of competency you will embed into your training programs.

ACTIVITY: Competency Development

1. List 10 task skills your online course will deliver.

---

2. List 10 task management skills that your online course will deliver.

---

3. List 10 task contingency skills your online course will deliver.

---

4. List 10 role specific task skills your online course will deliver.

PLAN YOUR COURSE SPECIFICATIONS

This isn't the sexiest part of course creation, but it's extremely important for those who wish to deliver high quality training programs. And it's critical for those who are building a serious education-based business. It's all in the details, and as a seasoned education provider, I can confidently say that if you get these things right in the first place, they can save all kinds of headaches later on, not only from a quality and standardised delivery point of view, but also from an operational, managerial and customer experience point of view.

In earlier chapters, we planned the *what's and why's* behind your course. We considered how we might deliver our training to make it engaging for the adult learner. We even gave the course a name, learning outcomes and a written description. Now we will continue to build on these basic details to make a thorough foundation to build a quality course upon.

Create module descriptions and outcomes

Creating great content and learning experiences for our online courses starts with knowing precisely what results we are trying to provide to our learners. This means that effective training design doesn't have just one single set of learning outcomes. It means breaking apart every element of the training program and identifying the objective of its constituent parts.

Your next task is to:

1. Write a description of the results each module will give your learners.
2. Create clearly defined, measurable learning outcomes for each module.

Consider industry regulatory or licensing requirements

Some industries require the learner or the trainer to hold certain licenses, tickets or qualifications to conduct certain tasks.

Prerequisites

Prerequisites are things that the learner must have, be, or do or, things that must happen before the training takes place.

What you might set as prerequisites for your training could be dictated by the industry you operate in, the accredited training requirements (if your training is accredited), the skill level required by their job roles and whatever terms you decide are entry requirements in order to start your training program and get the maximum benefit from it.

Other examples of prerequisites could include:

- how much experience the student already needs to have
- previous training they need to have
- certain level of skill or knowledge
- language and literacy ability
- certain level of health
- certain levels of eyesight, hearing or physical fitness

- certain equipment or resources that they need to have

Will your learners need to meet any prerequisites before joining your courses?

Evidence of Competence

This part of the training preparation process is about planning and documenting specifically how you will collect evidence that learners are gaining the required skills and knowledge, and are progressing towards the learning outcomes and that your program is working.

If you are delivering accredited training, this bit is going to be mostly done for you, as training packages have already pre-set performance and knowledge criteria, evidence requirements and assessment conditions that have been developed by the industry, training providers, skills councils and approved by the regulatory body, and as such, these conditions cannot be altered.

When developing non-accredited training, we can exponentially benefit by taking cues from accredited training to inform our practical and assessment elements, as they clearly and explicitly determine specifications around:

- the exact skills a learner will be able to perform
- the exact knowledge they will be able to prove they have acquired
- The exact type and amount of evidence that must be collected to back up and justify that the skills and knowledge have been met

Sarah Cordiner

- the definitions, benchmarks and parameters of what competence will look like

We can take advantage of these frameworks to inform our own non-accredited training. For example, if you head over to the Australian qualification registry, www.training.gov.au, you can search for nationally recognised training, pull up these detailed guidelines, and then adapt them for your own quality delivery. Just keep in mind that you may not, under any circumstances, claim to deliver accredited training unless you are an approved registered training organisation or legally partnered with one. This method is to inform and guide your practise, not to copy training packages entirely or make any fraudulent claims.

Another way to assess learner progress and collect evidence of competence is to create assessments around your own defined learning outcomes.

Assessments can come in many forms, formal and informal, and they can be direct, indirect and supplementary.

Here are some examples of ways that you could collect evidence to get your thinking hats on:

Methods	Example of sources of evidence
Observation	Real work activities at the workplace or in the live environment Demonstration of work activities Role-play performance Video recording of performance

Questioning	Verbal or written answers to questions
Review of products	Work samples 'Things' created by the learner
Portfolio	A collection of documentation Procedures completed Training records Personal documents, e.g. resumes, reflections Examples of workplace documents
Third-party report	Reports or formal documentation from someone else
Structured activities	Project Case Study Presentations Essays Exams Tests Quizzes

Definitions, Range Statements and Variations

Just like any thorough and quality conscious business has terms and conditions for their products and services, education providers should have clearly defined definitions, terms and conditions around how the training will be delivered and assessed, for all the stakeholders involved.

Ensure that expectations of the outcomes are completely

explicit by providing clear definitions of what each key term means in a glossary of definitions, with no room for vagueness whatsoever.

Have statement definitions that explain to what extent variations, adaptations and customisation may be made to assessment and evidence conditions so that there is no ambiguity around what is expected of learners

ACTIVITY: Collecting Evidence

1. How will you gather evidence to check that your learners are gaining competence?

2. What methods of formal or informal assessment will you use?

3. What kinds of special assessments do you need to create?

PREPARE FOR STAKEHOLDERS

In this section, we're going to look at who your stakeholders are, and why and how they influence the training design and delivery process.

Who are your stakeholders?

Depending on what you are teaching and under what circumstances, there is a limitless possibility of who your stakeholders might be. However, in general, a stakeholder is any individual, group of individuals or organisation that is either directly impacted by the training or has some form of investment in it in the means of finances, time, resources or emotion. This could include:

- Target learner groups
- Individual learners
- Candidates for assessment
- Organisations or businesses paying for the training
- Government bodies and agencies

Who are the stakeholders of your learning program?

Stakeholders are people who have any kind of involvement in the training delivery process. This could be your students themselves, or the client that you're delivering for.

Who is receiving the learning is a stakeholder, but also whoever is paying for the learning is a stakeholder. You could have many other external stakeholders involved. The trainer may not necessarily be the assessor. There may be a number of trainers depending on the different aspects and requirements of the program. They are all stakeholders too.

Depending on the size and the location of your program, there may also be a number of different people who are involved in the program process and operation itself. This could be employers if it's work-based learning. There could be managers or supervisors involved, who have to report on the students' progress.

Administrators are also stakeholders, as they may need to communicate with learners, instructors and workplaces as part of the successful completion of the training program.

Then there are those stakeholders who are more out of sight, but are just as significant, as their requirements can influence every aspect of the training design, delivery, record keeping, pricing, duration and more. These kinds of stakeholders could include the government, regulatory bodies, licensing authorities and organisations who are stakeholders. If you have equipment that's used as part of your training process, the people who inspect, maintain and check the equipment safety are stakeholders.

I hope that this shows you how training programs involve far more than just the trainer and the learner. You have to consider stakeholders at all phases of the training design and delivery, including the delivery, assessment, management and maintenance.

Much of this can cause complications and a little extra work at times, but it's also a really great thing because we can incorporate the experience, expertise, knowledge and collaboration of all of these people to help us ensure a highly effective program. After all, as stakeholders, it is in all their interests to ensure the program is a success.

If you're just developing training for yourself, or for your own online private courses, consider the fact that you likely have stakeholders, too. There could be the online learning platforms that you're using. You still have all of your learners, the group of learners as a unit and the industry that you're working in.

Regardless of how many or what kind of stakeholders you have involved in your training programs, planning how this will impact your training design and delivery before you get started on building your course is vital.

ACTIVITY: Stakeholder Planning

1. Who are your stakeholders?

2. How so your stakeholders impact your learners and their learning?

3. How will your design of the course need to be adjusted to consider stakeholders?

PLAN FOR STAKEHOLDER NEEDS

When it comes to building and delivering your training program, the needs of your stakeholders are very important considerations for you to make. These needs could be endless depending on the types of stakeholders that you might have involved.

Below is a list of some of the considerations that we need to make about the things that affect our stakeholders when it comes to building our program.

You will need to work make a list of questions for your stakeholders and conduct a guided consultation using the considerations listed below to ensure that your program will effectively meet the needs of everyone involved.

Consider the following as discussion or question areas when building your course:

- industry or vocational focus
- learner career options or ambitions
- learner or organisational background
- budgets
- purpose of the training and assessment
- previous experience
- previous formal learning
- time or season constraints
- special needs
- location, geography and venues
- gaps, problems and issues the training is to address
- goals, objectives or results the training drives toward

ACTIVITY: Stakeholder Needs

In addition to coming up with as many questions as you can around the key stakeholders' needs listed above, now answer these questions:

1. Write a brief description of your potential clients and stakeholders of your training program.

2. Describe your target learner group and their characteristics.

3. Are any of the above likely to have special needs or requirements that should be addressed?

4. Are they looking for advanced learning, or are they complete beginners?

5. Do they understand industry terminology, or is it all new to them?

6. Using the list above, write a list of questions you may need to ask your stakeholders in order to confirm and meet their requirements, desires and expectations.

THE LEARNING PRINCIPLE OF LEARNER-CENTRED EDUCATION

Teacher-centered education is training that is designed and delivered in a way that the teacher holds the power in the learning environment. It is all about the teacher passing their knowledge onto the learners in a didactic manner while the learners remain mostly passive as listeners in the learning experience.

Learner-centered education has an appropriate balance of communication, influence and control over the learning experience. The teacher acts more as a facilitator and nurtures explorative and collaborative learning.

There are good and bad places to use each style. Learner-centered education may be less effective in a situation where there is a high risk to life, environment and equipment. If performed incorrectly, it would need to be highly controlled by an instructor to ensure the safety and effectiveness of the learning experience. And there are other situations when the teacher-centered approach would be stifling to all learning.

As you are designing your own training programs, please consider how learner- or teacher-centered your training needs to be in order to be effective and facilitate the optimum educational experience for your learners.

Here is a table that gives an overview of the major differences in teacher-centered and learner-centered education so that you can decide what mixture is best for your training.

Teacher-Centered	Learner-Centered
It's all about the trainer.	There is a balance between focus on the trainer and the learners.
It's about how much the trainer knows, can do, has done. All examples are about the trainer's experiences and stories.	All examples are contextualised to something the learner can directly relate to or may have experienced themselves.
Trainer talks and the learners listen.	There is interaction between the trainer and the learners.
Language used is about the trainer's knowledge of that language.	Language used is typical of the language the learners would use every day in the environment they are training for.
Learners work alone.	Learners work alone as well as collaboratively with others.
Trainer monitors and corrects all learner contributions.	Learners talk, discuss and communicate their thoughts freely, and the trainer only provides feedback or correction when required.

The trainer answers all questions.	The learners answer each other's questions and use the trainer as a facilitator or resource for the interactions.
Trainer makes all of the decisions about the learning journey.	The learners can influence and contribute to the training design and learning experience.
The trainer is responsible for all assessment and evaluations of learning.	The learners evaluate and self-assess their own progression, as well as the trainer.
The learning environment is often quiet and controlled.	Learning environment can be noisy and busy.

There is no formal right or wrong on this. As discussed, the topic, the environment, the learners and the objectives of the training will all determine which approach is most suitable. But from a personal perspective, the learner-centered approach offers a 'best of both worlds' outcome with a balance between the trainer and learner all gaining the best from one another.

ACTIVITY: Be Learner-Centred

1. What do the learners need to be able to do themselves?

2. Is it better for them to practice this or for you to tell them about it?

3. Will giving them the definitions and answers help them best, or will they gain more by having to explore and discover the answers for themselves?

4. Are there considerations such as safety that require you to be in control of all elements of the training, or could more be gained by allowing flexibility and influence from the learners?

IDENTIFY TARGET LEARNER GROUP NEEDS

> Different learners =

>> Different characteristics =

>>> Different range of support and delivery options

When it comes to planning and designing effective adult learning programs, it is important that we clearly understand who our target group of adult learners actually are so that we can design the training to meet the group's needs, and as we will discuss later, their individual needs, too.

When it comes to thinking about your target group, it is important to remember that different learners have very different characteristics. They have very different learning preferences, learning modes and learning styles. They work and live in very different environments and come from very different backgrounds, which means that the way we have to design and deliver our training needs to vary from group to group, as well as down to the individual level, as far as it is possible.

To design and deliver excellent training, we cannot just have one single plan for delivery. We need to have an entire toolbox of resources, methods and approaches that we can draw upon to cater for every mix of group needs we might face.

These means that we need to gather the best possible picture and avatar of our group as a whole.

ACTIVITY: Know the Generalisation of Your Group

The characteristics of your target learner groups need to be taken into account. Think about each of the following and draw up a profile of your learners using these prompts:

- level and breadth of work experience
- level and previous experiences of formal education
- skill or competency profile
- socioeconomic background
- cultural background and needs
- age
- gender
- special needs
- motivation for learning
- language, literacy and numeracy needs
- learning styles and preferences
- whether they qualify for training as determined by a funding body, based on criteria such as residence and length of time in the country they live in, length of time unemployed, etc.
- specific levels of English language, literacy and numeracy skills as determined by initial assessment process

IDENTIFY INDIVIDUAL LEARNER NEEDS

When we're planning the design and delivery of our training, we also need to think about our individual learner needs as well as that of the group.

These include all of the considerations we would make when planning training around an entire group as discussed in the chapter above, but we would try as far as possible to address these at an individual level.

In addition to the factors considered in the previous chapter, we may also consider factors at an individual level, such as the following:

- occupational status
- access to equipment and resources
- physical or psychological abilities
- level of maturity
- religious and spiritual beliefs

Once you have a clear idea of the general group as a whole, you can do your best to collect as much data as possible and think as deeply as possible about every individual who will be part of your program. Then ask yourself:

How can I tailor this learning to these individual's needs, to their background, to their specifications, to their motivations, to their life experience, to their work experience, to the place and context in which they're going to take this learning?

The more you think about the individual, the more you're going to increase the enjoyment, the outcome and the impact of the learning experience itself.

ACTIVITY: Know Every Individual Need

Now dig much deeper and think about each person that is most likely to find themselves in your training courses.

Again, use the prompts below to come up with a number of learner avatars that will enable you to plan your training design and delivery to meet as many as possible.

- work or life application / why they are doing the training
- occupational status
- access to equipment and resources
- physical or psychological disability
- Language Literacy and Numeracy (You might need to employ a LLN for this analysis.)
- employment status
- learning experiences
- work experiences
- level of maturity
- cultural background
- level of formal schooling
- length of time as a resident
- place of residence

PLAN FOR COURSE CREATION IN CORPORATE AND WORKPLACE TRAINING

What factors can influence the design and delivery of our online and offline courses in a workplace environment?

In reality this list could be endless, but when it comes to corporate, work-based or vocational training, there are some top-of-the-list factors that all course creators and instructors should very carefully consider, as each can have a considerable impact on every element of the program.

Factor #1: National Training Frameworks and Accreditation Requirements

If you're delivering an accredited course, then the primary consideration you need to make, and the number one influence of your program design, is going to be the requirements of the accreditation and training framework to which it belongs. If you're following a specified training package or licensed content, then you must make sure that you're following the guidelines, criteria, requirements, conditions and compliance standards of the training package or qualification package that you're following. That will form the fundamentals of your training program itself, how it's going to be delivered, the duration and a whole host of different requirements that are going to impact that the way the course is actually designed.

Factor #2: Employee Location, Physical Availability and Impact on Daily Operations

Will your training be delivered entirely online? Will your

learners need to travel? Will the training require them to take time off work, or slow down operations for themselves and their supervisors if the training takes place in a live working environment? Knowing exactly how location and context will affect your training is a critical component to your training design process.

Factor #3: Prerequisites and Entry Requirements

Your training program design and delivery will be affected if you have learners enroll who do not posses preexisting skills. For example, you may require learners to have a certain level of language and literacy skills, a particular measure of eyesight or even preexisting qualifications, licences or years of experience.

If you have an audience that is rather low in terms of its ability to read, write and articulate, clearly that's going to significantly influence the way that you write the program compared to if you had a highly academic group of learners.

Factor #4: Prior Learning and Experience

Knowing what skills, experience, knowledge and competence a learner brings with them into your training course will enable you to plan for training that is more effective.

Aside from ensuring that your training course will meet the learning outcomes, knowing your learners prior educational and work experiences will help you determine how you will deliver your content. If your learners arrive to your training with significant experience in your topic, then you may deliver that content at a surface level more than if it was their first time studying your topic.

Factor #5: Specified Competency Requirements for Safe Working Practices

The requirements of a training package will have enormous influence on your training program design and delivery.

The skills, knowledge, competency and assessment requirements stipulated by training packages will dominate the entire course creation process, from the type of content we are producing to the educational level, even precisely how it must be delivered and assessed in order to be compliant, let alone effective.

For some courses, you might just deliver information and knowledge. That might more straightforward, faster and easier to deliver in videos or in self-paced 'self-study' type planning than if you had a course that was focussed on the practical implementation of technical skills that required equipment and resources.

If you have to meet training package requirements as part of your training, or at least design training that will be aligned to accredited training to be competitive, it could mean having to design extended practical training elements, log nominal hours and employ qualified assessors in order to practice that skill.

Factor #6: Company Policies and Procedures

When training is being delivered for or in a workplace, the procedures, policies and rules in that environment will have a significant impact on your training design and delivery. Are there special procedures that they must follow when managing tasks, operating machinery or equipment, reporting issues, dealing with paperwork and communicating with other colleagues?

Try to get hold of the standard operating procedures of the workplace that will be affected by your training, and use their procedures as contextualisation. Encourage the learners to contextualise their own training by sourcing procedures and policies from their own workplace environments as part of their activities.

Factor #7: Standard Operating Procedures

Standard operating procedures are the step-by-step process that a specific work environment, business, industry or country specifies that a task should be correctly conducted by. If your training program requires your learners to use a piece of equipment (this could be anything from a stapler to an excavator), that equipment may come with special procedures or operating processes that have to be followed when conducting or using that equipment safely.

Your training program would need to be built around the guidelines or operating manual that may come with it. Again, you can see how this would affect the way you are going to design and deliver your training program.

Factor #8: Regulatory, Legal and Licensing Requirements

Regulatory and licensing requirements in an industry or country will impact your training design and delivery.

Obviously, laws and legislation come in for a whole host of reasons, not just the environment that we're in. Perhaps the industry that we're training in or indeed the types of task that the student is going to have to go on and perform can all influence the training design as well. If we're delivering something that's attached to a license of some kind, then clearly we're going to make sure we design our training around the requirements, the performance criteria and the standards of that particular license.

This is not a full list of considerations by far, but it does provide the most common factors that can impact your training design and delivery. If you want to build the best training in a vocational setting, make sure you have a significant planning phase around addressing these criteria.

DETERMINE THE LEARNING TIMEFRAMES

Time is a very big consideration when it comes to designing, developing and delivering our training. Face-to-face and group learning can be more time consuming than self-paced online learning (depending on how it's delivered, how much detail you go into and how you have developed your schedule).

A number of factors may affect the amount of time that is available for the learning process, and even the design process! This stage is about considering all of the time-affecting variables so that our training courses will be effective.

The time spent on each element of the learning program will ultimately influence what your learning program covers, the extent of detail it will cover and how it will be broken down into sections or chunks to enhance learning

When planning your training program, consider:

- Nominal hours
- Client specified timeframes
- Your suggested timeframes or different depths of learning
- Your prior experience in designing learning programs and delivering training
- Involvement and availability of other stakeholders

1.Client specifications

Your clients, learners or customers may specify a certain training duration. For example, I have had clients come to me many times and say, "*We would like a 1-day course on XXX.*"

The client's timeframe could be affected by a need to have skills developed by a certain deadline or a certain period in which they have to learn the training. It may be that there is only a certain amount of downtime that the students are allowed to have from work, or because they think the time will affect the cost. Don't forget to quiz the learner or the customer on why they have specified a date, as it could be that their lack of knowledge around the training design and delivery process has initiated the request rather than there being a need for that time duration. We only want necessity to affect the learning experience, not naivety.

2. Industry guidelines

Industry guidelines, such as nominal hours can have a huge impact on the design and delivery of your training program. Nominal hours are normally government-endorsed industry guidelines that specify the amount of practical and theory training, how many hours or days of training and in what context the learner must do them in order to gain sufficient competence. Clearly, if you have developed a 3-day training course and then discover that your industry recommends a minimum of 3-months training with a 6-month practical work experience placement, then your course is likely to be uncompetitive and even redundant.

For instance, in some licence-based or accredited training, the practice and training hours must be recorded in a formal (and legal) log book and signed off by certified practitioners, in order for the industry to deem them as having had sufficient training experience. If your training has not been designed to meet these conditions, you are not going to have a very profitable training business.

3. Course development time

Another time consideration is not just the face-to-face or online learning time that might be available to the student, but it also could be things like the amount of time you need to develop the training itself.

- How much content do you already have?
- How many tasks need to be built from scratch?
- How much can be built by you or the team, that you currently have available, and how much of that would need to be influenced or contributed to by technical or subject matter experts?

Keep in mind, also, that if you require subject matter experts, auditors or review teams to be involved in your course creation process, then this too will add time on to your project line. Not to mention that they may need to fit that contribution in around a certain schedule of their own, or other work commitments that they have.

Make your timelines for both delivery of your training and the design of it in the first place an important element of your training planning process.

ACTIVITY: Planning Your Program Timeframes

1. How long do they need to adequately learn, acquire and take on the skills, knowledge, competencies that you're passing onto them?

2. How much time do the learners and the clients have available?

3. What are their expectations?

4. Are they expecting to do a one-hour course, or are they expecting a twelve-month, in-depth learning program?

5. Do we have to consider any industry standards in terms of nominal hours?

6. Are there any guided logbook timelines that we need to consider and incorporate into the training and design delivery?

7. What about individual needs or geography?

8. Are you getting people who are coming into your program nationally or internationally?

9. Are you bringing together a group for two or three day programs? Are you travelling the world on tour to take your training to your learners, or are you planning a self-study course that is completely online?

10. Will you be delivering synchronistic or asynchronistic training?

11. Is it a one off one-day program? Or is it a week-long program?

12. If it is a multiple-day program? Will it be delivered in one solid block, or will the training days be separated over a period of time?

13. Is it self-paced or teacher-led?

14. Will there be a drip-released content feature that will affect the delivery schedule?

15. Will your training be a blended learning approach, which will involve different types of time considerations depending on the medium of delivery at each part of the training schedule?

Answering these questions will help you with planning when it comes to putting your course's timeframe together.

Write down these answers now before you move on.

CONCLUSION

Adult education, most commonly referred to as 'andragogy,' is a continuously changing concept, and the landscape in which it is applied is forever changing with it. Having recently experienced a learning revolution with the sudden surge of online learning, we are seeing more opportunities to learn and teach than ever, all at a huge reduction of the price and without having to leave our own homes.

This has opened up a global marketplace for edupreneurs and brings with it the benefit of changing lives and contributing to our industry in a way that benefits everyone. We are shifting rapidly into a world where equal access to creating, delivering and accessing education is within reach of billions of people.

With the plethora of benefits and good that this brings, it has also seen a rapid dilution in the quality of training programs. Traditional teacher training and curriculum design principles are going un-delivered to edupreneurs, and the education industry is being infiltrated by inexperienced marketers and money-grabbing trend-riders all of whom claim to teach edupreneurs how to 'make it' in the education sector without any consideration whatsoever to the learners experience or the principles of adult learning; which are critical to creating training that is of any use.

Training will forever evolve, and none of us can ever truly be entirely on top of all of the best practices for educational design. It is critical that we address the issue of quality training design for those who have not been educationally trained so that everyone can develop, deliver and receive thoroughly planned, engaging, quality and effective training, in whatever way they consume it.

In this book, I have presented numerous timeless and new age considerations, theories, strategies and principles of formal curriculum design and delivery to enable the modern day edupreneur to be equipped with the most fundamental of underpinning knowledge to develop quality training programs that will serve their learners, their industry and themselves.

The characteristics of adult learning differ from the learning of children in that it is said to be self-directed, experiential, oriented, requires relevance and immediate application, and can be influenced by a number of motivations as well as the context in which the learning is taking place.

The level of importance, the ratio of each, and the time in one's life that education should occur is largely contested, and no exact model has yet been produced suggesting the best approaches and teaching methods in the field of adult learning.

However, by using the theories, models and frameworks of adult education within this book, adult educators can create more effective training today, from which they can derive their own philosophies and practices.

Like Knowles (1984), I have deeply held beliefs that adult education requires a large degree of self-direction. In situations where learners are forced to take a certain educational path, negative learning experiences are more frequently reported.

Allowing learners the freedom to express themselves, lead their own learning journey and subsequently learn a great deal about themselves through reflection on their development, the learning process is significantly enhanced.

When learning is too directed, I fear learners will not be provided with sufficient opportunity for risk-taking and therefore will make constructive mistakes. However, we must still recognise the importance of guidance and the need for structured direction, especially in situations where a large amount of information must be relayed.

In terms of context, there is more to allowing for learning than simply making sure the room is warm enough, for example. A thorough consideration for learners' feelings, external issues they may have, and establishing group agreements on classroom conduct are essential in creating a positive and productive learning environment.

The past experiences an adult has had throughout his life, the positive and negative influences that this can bring to the classroom, the social place they feel they have in the situation, their motives for being in the class, and what they feel they will get out of being part of it will all affect how they approach the educational experience.

Their past experiences will also affect how much they learn from your training and how they will approach education in the future. Subsequently, this means that it also impacts what you need to do to design and deliver an effective learning experience.

Although the concepts, frameworks and theory of creating effective adult learning programs presented in this book are not entirely exhaustive, my aim is to have provided the quality-conscious and ethical edupreneur with the fundamental principles, practices and considerations of adult learning design and delivery in a way that further informs their approach to all aspects of planning, developing, teaching and learning to create more effective training courses for everyone.

CONNECT WITH SARAH

Join the community. Share your questions, thoughts and stories with Sarah here: www.sarahcordiner.com

Join Sarah's Facebook Group: *Entrepreneur to Edupreneur – Course Creators:*
www.sarahcordiner.com/FacebookGroup

Connect with Sarah on LinkedIn:
www.sarahcordiner.com/LinkedIn

Follow andTweet Sarah Cordiner on Twitter:
@CordinerSarah

Like Sarah on Facebook:
www.facebook.com/CordinerSarah

Subscribe to Sarah's YouTube channel:
www.sarahcordiner.com/YouTube

Connect with Sarah on Instagram:

www.instagram.com/maintraining/

ABOUT THE AUTHOR

I help you create and sell your own engaging and profitable training courses.

"You have unique talents, knowledge, skills and competencies just waiting to be unlocked. It doesn't matter what your starting point is, or how little you have – with a little bit of resourcefulness, the gift of self-efficacy and some good education, everything you dream of is possible."

Sarah Cordiner

Qualified educational entrepreneur.

Sarah is a Number 1 Best-Selling Author in Education & Business. She is a qualified trainer, professional speaker and respected consultant in Edupreneurship, Edu-marketing, Entrepreneurship, Workforce Development, Curriculum Development, Instructional Design, Education and Training and online learning. She is a specialist in training development and curriculum design, as well as trainer of trainers in adult learning.

- CEO of MainTraining
- Co-Director of 'The Training Revolution' (Virtual Reality Education & Training)
- PGCE in Adult Education; BA (Hons) in Education; Diploma in Lifelong Learning; TAE40110 Cert IV in Training & Assessment
- Television Presenter of the 'Course Creators' show on www.BRiN.ai
- Listed by the Huffington Post as one of the 'Top 50 Must-Follow Female Entrepreneurs for 2017'
- Owner and Host of 'The Course Creators Podcast' on iTunes
- Diploma in Business; Diploma in Leadership & Management
- Winner of the 'Influential 100 Awards 2015 and 2016'
- Founder of 'The Edupreneur Awards'
- Finalist of the Telstra Young Business Woman of the Year 2015
- Finalist of the Telstra Start-Up Business of the Year 2015
- Ranked the Global 'Top 4 e-Learning Blog' in 2016

Sarah's Keynote and Expert Topics:

Sarah delivers international bootcamps on online course creation, filming, editing and online course marketing: www.sarahcordiner.com/CourseWhisperers

Keynote:
Capitalising on the Global Online Learning & Ed-Tech Revolution

- How to dramatically increase your international presence by tapping into billion dollar learning marketplaces
- How to re-purpose and diversify your training offerings to increase revenue streams, course enrollments, sales and profits
- How to lead in the VET (Vocational Education and Training) industry by offering your training in the newest and most revolutionary form of training delivery

General Topics Tailored To Audience:

- Online Course Creation as a Business
- Vocational Education & Training
- Engaging Teaching & Learning Practices
- Curriculum/Instructional Design and Development
- Creating Profitable Courses and Training Programs
- Creating Online Learning Programs
- Marketing and Sales of Education and Training Programs
- Making Training Businesses More Profitable -

Ethically
- Entrepreneurship & Business Start-Up Success Strategies
- Edupreneurship: What entrepreneurs and businesses in any industry can learn about growing business by using the platform of education instead of sales, and how to create profitable learning products and programs as a lead generation tool
- Workforce Planning & Development: How large businesses and corporate enterprises can maximise their productivity and profitability by effectively utilising and developing their workforce skills and capabilities
- Profitable Workforce Development: Staff Training for Positive ROI
- Students Transitioning from Education to Employment: What's next and what do employers really want?
- The Student's Formula For Success
- Overcoming Adversity: How actively creating adversity as well as effectively coping with it is the key to success in life and business

Sarah's work has enabled the education of thousands of professional workers and business owners in over 120 countries towards their personal and professional goals.

Her training has helped welfare dependents in remote Australian communities (and throughout the UK) progress to employment. She initiated the movement of 'Edupreneurship' and assisted other training providers to deliver excellent training via her train-the-trainer programs, consultancy and training design and development services, and has even supported the economic development of entire communities by providing training and consultancy on training and workforce development initiatives.

Sarah's (very brief) story!

I am a 'rags to riches', 'anything is possible' and the 'just get off your behind and make it happen' educational entrepreneur.

When I first started in business in the UK at nineteen years old, I had zero business training, $17 in my bank account and loved ones telling me I was stupid.

Hailing from a gypsy background where female education and entrepreneurship was frowned upon, my dreams had been crushed and ridiculed. I started an education business anyway where my competition was the Federal Government and two multi-million dollar global enterprises. But my passion could move planets. So I did it anyway, and I succeeded.

In 2012, my circumstances dramatically changed, and I washed up on the shores of Western Australia–no money, friends, phone, laptop or bed to sleep in. Eighteen months later, I'm recognised as a leader in my industry. I have twenty-three people working for me, and I have turned down an offer of $3 *million for my business. Add 3.5 years to that and one of the most prestigious business magazines has listed me as one of the 'Top 50 Must Follow Female Entrepreneurs for 201.' I have my own TV show, and I am a multi-award winning, two-time international number 1 best-*

selling author, with a blog listed in the top 4 in the world in my industry. Not bad for a homeless gypsy.

My education services business 'MainTraining' has now been in operation for over a decade. I teach thousands (including international enterprises, prisoners, long-term unemployed, schools, colleges, universities, defence forces, remote communities, governments, corporate professionals, international franchises and entrepreneurs) in over 120 countries.

I now speak on international stages about lifelong/vocational education, edupreneurship, course creation, business, and marketing. I'm booked up to two years in advance. I've gone from desperately handing out my email address on scraps of stolen paper, to having over 50,000 followers on my email database and social media combined.

I am inspired by those 'normal' people who have achieved their goals through hard work and passion. Having now done the same, I want to make sure no dream goes unrealised. My goal is to show 10 million current or aspiring entrepreneurs, business owners, edupreneurs and professionals by 2020, that no matter your circumstances, who you are or where your starting point is, you CAN make anything happen if you try hard enough and put the right strategies into play.

If you would like to book Sarah as a speaker, trainer or presenter at your next event, or book a consultation, please contact her on sarah@sarahcordiner.com

ABOUT SARAH'S COMPANY: MainTraining

www.maintraining.com.au

MainTraining is an international training delivery and curriculum design and development company.

MainTraining provides the following services:

1. Online Course Creation Services
2. Online School Set Up Services
3. Delivery of Training, Education & Qualifications – we deliver a range of personal and professional development training to businesses, individuals, Government, remote communities
4. Curriculum Design and Development - planning the structure of your training products and programs, creating learning outcomes, developing module content plans and lesson plans for accredited and non-accredited training.
5. Researching & Developing - the content for your training/learning product or program; creating PowerPoint slides, Prezi slides, learner workbooks, assessments, quizzes, how-to guides and other educational content.
6. Developing Learning Content and resources for accredited training, to be compliant with regulatory authority requirements or regulated curriculum (such as for registered training organisations, universities, colleges, schools, licensed training and high-risk training).
7. Converting face to face training into online learning or creating e-learning and online courses from

scratch and setting up your online school for you.
8. Online Course and Edu-Business Marketing - We help you create and maximise your training course sales, exposure and lead generation with content re-purposing and specialist education marketing advice.
9. Virtual Reality Educational Design - We convert your current training (accredited or non-accredited) into a virtual reality curriculum.
10. Online course creation & online school set up - Everything from planning out your online course plan, to setting up and branding your online school, integrating all of your software with your school filming, film editing, uploading your content and helping you market your online courses, too.
11. 9.Training administration services –
    Training document formatting, editing, PowerPoint presentation creation and editing.

Visit www.maintraining.com.au for more information and quotes.

REFERENCES

Belanger, P. (1996). 'Trends in Adult Education Policy'. Adult Education and Development, 47

Brookfield, S. D. (1986) Understanding and Facilitating Adult Learning. A comprehensive analysis of principles and effective practice, Milton Keynes: Open University Press

Brysk, A. (2003). 'Globalization and Human Rights: It's a small world after all'. Phi Kappa, Phi Forum, 83

Boud, D. et al (1985) Reflection. Turning experience into learning, London: Kogan Page.

Dunn, R., & Griggs, S. (1998). Learning styles: Link between teaching and learning. In Dunn, R., & Griggs (Eds.), Learning styles and the nursing profession (pp. 11-23). New York: NLN Press.

Erikson, E & Piaget, J. (1982) Profile of Three Theories. Kendall Hunt Pub Co.

Conflicius (45oBC) quote from hgp://reviewing.co.uk/research/-experiential.learning Accessed 6th March 2008

Conner, M. L. 'How Adults Learn.' Ageless Learner, 1997-2007. Available at: http://agelessleamer.com/intros/adultlearninghtml Date accessed 01.03.2008

Coombes, P.and Ahmed, M. (1974). Attacking Rural Poverty. Baltimore: Johns Hopkins University Press.

Dave, R. (1976). Foundations of Lifelong Education, Oxford: Pergamon Press. (for UNESCO institute for Education).

Dewey, J. (1916) Education and Democracy. New York: The Free Press

Dewey, J. (1933) How We Think, New York: D. C. Heath.

Fencl, H and Scheel, K Sep 2005 Journal of College Science Teaching v. 35, issue 1, p. 20-24

Glastra, F, Hake, B. & Schedler, P. (2004) 'Lifelong Learning as -Transitional Learning'. Adult Education Quaterly. 54.

Jarvis, P. (1987) Adult Learning in the Social Context. London: Croom Helm

Jarvis, P. (2004) Adult Education and Lifelong Learning: Theory and Practice. USA, Routledge Falmer.

Kegan, R. (2000). What "form" Transforms? A Constructive-developmental perspective on transformative learning. In J. Mezirow & Associates, Learning as Transformation: Critical Perspectives on a theory in progress. San-Francisco: Jossey-Bass

Knowles, M. (1984). The Adult Learner: A Neglected Species (3rd Ed.). Houston, TX: Gulf Publishing

Lieb, S (199]) Principles of adult learning. Vison, Arizona. [ONLINE] available at www.about.corn, date accessed 01.03.2008

Maslow, A (1943) 'A Theory of Human Motivation', Psychological Review 50 370-96.

Merriam, S; Caffarella, R and Baumgartner, L. (2007). Learning in Adulthood: A Comprehensive Guide. San Francisco : Jossey-Bass

M.S. Knowles, "Self-Directed Learning", A Guide for Learners and Teachers. (N.Y. Cambridge Books 1975) p.18

Schunk, Dale H; Pajares Frank, 2002 Academic Press in A. Wigfield and J. Eccles (Eds), Development of Achievement Motivation

Shovlin, C, (2005) Museums, Libraries and Archives Council, London. [ONLINE] Available at: http://wwwmla.gov.uk/resources/assets, date accessed 01.03.2008

Smith, M. K. (1996; 1999) 'Andragogy', the encyclopaedia of informal education, http://www.infed.org[lifelongleaminglb-andra.htm date accessed

Smith, RM. (1991). How people become effective learners. Adult Learning, p. 11. Available at: http://agelessleamer.com/intros/adultleaming date accessed 1 March 2008

Taylor, EW. (2005) Making meaning of the varied and contested perspectives on transformative learning theory: In D. Vlosak et al: Proceedings of the 6" International conference on Transformative Learning. East Lansing: Michigan State University.

Tennant, MC. (1988). Psychology and adult Learning. New York: -Routledge.

Zemke, R & S (1984). '30 things we know for sure about adult -learning'. Innovation

Abstracts Vol VI, No 8, March 9, available at: hgpM/adultedaboutcom, date accessed 01.03.2008

THE BLURB

It is no secret that the online learning industry is booming. But with a mass influx of course creators and marketers jumping into the 'educational gold rush' to make money, the critical components of developing *quality* and *effective* training are being lost.

Anyone can create and sell online courses to a global marketplace today, at minimal expense and from their own spare rooms – which is a great thing for everyone. However, if you aspire to create *transformational* online or face to face training programs that engage and enrich your learners; it is vital that you design and develop your programs with the fundamental theory and principles of adult learning and course creation in mind. Training that does not satisfy your learners, or follow quality educational practices, will attract negative reviews, a bad reputation and refund requests – something that no course creator or 'edupreneur' wants to face.

With the learning industry becoming a rapidly more competitive field, survival in this lucrative market is about creating remarkable training that has the learner experience at its core.

This book has been especially designed by multiple-award winning, qualified education professional, Sarah Cordiner for the modern day, quality-conscious course creator, edupreneur and training manager who cares about their learner experience. It is for those who want to plan, prepare and deliver transformational training that changes the lives of those that they teach.

By presenting timeless theories, principles, frameworks, processes and practices for designing, developing and delivering highly effective training programs, this book will help you create learning that will positively impact your learners - and your business.

FREE ECOURSE:

Get Sarah Cordiner's best-selling online course *'How to Create Profitable Courses'* for FREE as a thank you for purchasing this book: www.sarahcordiner.com/BookBonus

GET A SECOND COURSE FOR FREE

Would you like to get Sarah's online course *'The Course Marketing Masterclass'* for FREE?

How to get your free course marketing course:

1. Go to Facebook and 'like' my Sarah Cordiner page. Here is a link directly to my Facebook page (www.sarahcordiner.com/Facebook)
2. Take a picture of yourself with this book.
3. Upload the picture of you and this book to Facebook and tag Sarah Cordiner.
4. Write what you liked about the book.
5. Set the privacy of your post to 'public'
6. We will reply to you privately with the free coupon link

Printed in Poland
by Amazon Fulfillment
Poland Sp. z o.o., Wrocław